JUST A NURSE

Hope Gravett qualified as a nurse in the 1950s and from then on, despite the pay and conditions, she found nursing a fulfilling career – and saw sides of life that most of us only have nightmares about. Brawling men needing stitches, a New Zealand family injured – and covered in soot – when a chimney fell on their holiday flat, a woman complaining that her backside was alight after a firework went up her skirt. Here are some of her amusing, dramatic and moving stories of her time on the wards and as a district nurse.

JUST A NURSE

JUST A NURSE

by

Hope Gravett

Dales Large Print Books
Long Preston, North Yorkshire,
BD23 4ND, England.

British Library Cataloguing in Publication Data.

Gravett, Hope
    Just a nurse.

    A catalogue record of this book is
    available from the British Library

    ISBN   1-84262-320-6 pbk

First published in Great Britain in 2003 by The Book Guild Ltd.

Copyright © Hope Gravett 2003

Cover illustration © Anthony Monaghan

The moral right of Hope Gravett to be identified as the author
of this work has been asserted by her in accordance with the
Copyright, Designs and Patents Act, 1988

Published in Large Print 2004 by arrangement with
The Book Guild Ltd.

Dales Large Print is an imprint of Library Magna Books Ltd.

Printed and bound in Great Britain by
T.J. (International) Ltd., Cornwall, PL28 8RW

CONTENTS

1

Nursing – First Time Round

This is not a conventional story of a girl who played with her dolls, and said that she wanted to be a nurse when she grew up, nor is it one of dedication so great that poor pay and conditions were accepted as normal in nursing. Eventually it was almost by chance that I got into a life which was to be fulfilling.

I had two goes at nursing training: one in a large children's hospital run by London County Council, a year or so before the outbreak of the Second World War; the second in 1953, when most of my contemporaries were well married and settled.

My mother had to accompany me to the interview for my first effort – imagine students tolerating that today! About a dozen of us stood eyeing one another as we waited for our interviews, which included a medical, to see whether our own GPs had been truthful. In those days everyone took it for granted that the lavatory had to be used periodically, but never talked about. So, imagine the stony silence and atmosphere when the home sister whispered to each one of us in turn, pointing to a curtained cubicle as she did so, and the embarrassment when the first poor girl could be heard doing what she'd been told to do! The remark I'd been going to make to reduce the tension died on my lips when I saw the expression on that sister's face.

Having been accepted for a month's provisional assessment, we said goodbyes to our mothers and went to be kitted out. Florence Nightingale would have been proud of the length of my uniform skirt and also of my first flush of nursing zeal. Getting used to communal food and living was the hardest thing for me, but luckily we all had single rooms, so my dread of sharing with a stranger didn't materialise, thank goodness.

My mother used to send me lovely parcels of home-made cakes, bread rolls, butter and any little things she could spare, by train in the morning, arriving at the hospital the same evening. They were the days of good railway services! On the parcel days my friends and I felt well-nourished.

The worst food I ever remember having was after I'd started ward work. The ward sister had kept me with her after we should have gone to supper, because a baby had died. This was shock enough, I'd never thought of a baby dying, not even a poor, pathetic, malformed one. When we had washed the baby and done all that was necessary in death, we went to the canteen. I was grudgingly handed a plate of a brown mixture, with potato and sad, over-boiled cabbage, and another plate of brown stuff with custard. After the first plateful, swallowed with difficulty because it was cold and I was upset, I started on the second, only to find it was custard on top of meat mixture instead of steamed pudding. It was so revolting I felt sick. Luckily the ward sister was still there and insisted that the server, to whom I was an utter nuisance, give me some of the cheese and biscuits reserved for the senior staff, so the revolting mess had been worth the nausea.

We had spent a month between the wards and lecture room before we started on the real training. My first evening on proper ward duty stands out in my memory after all these years. I had to take washing bowls to the biggest children who went to school in the grounds for part of each day, some on crutches, in plaster, surgical boots and other appliances – I'd not yet learned what they were called. At the end of afternoon school they all had to lie on their beds for a rest, but not undressed. Those who could get to the bath and washrooms did so, but most had to be given bowls. I'd given these out and then got a trolley with jugs of warm water to wheel round. One ten-year-old girl had a very fixed look in her blue eyes and as I turned to pour out her water, I saw she had only one eye, the other had gone! I was so startled I poured the water into the bed, not the bowl! With a shriek of triumph and in a strong cockney accent she said, 'That got yer, dint it, Nuss!' After changing the bed and tidying up generally I got the child to show me how her glass eye came out, was washed and replaced. My thirst for knowledge impressed her, and she became an ally, for woe betide any nurse to whom the children took exception; their lives were made a misery. I never imagined that the lesson given to me by a little cockney girl would come in useful to me years later. Once, when working as a district nurse, but first when I was coming home from years in India and had to replace a very elderly nun's glass eye that had fallen on the cabin floor and was covered in fluff!

Everyone had heard of infantile paralysis, many knew of deaths from it, and in this hospital were children permanently disabled from it. I learned then what a paralysed limb meant, the unpredictability of movement when one tried to get a floppy limb into socks, boots and callipers. The coldness of the limbs was unexpected, and a paralysed arm made a very good weapon lifted up by the other and plonked hard down on another's head.

Another lesson I learned was that parents never wanted to know anything at all critical of their children, and that unpalatable truths were couched in such terms by senior staff as to become untruths. I had a forthright lecture from a ward sister after a mother had complained that I said the others were frightened of her daughter. They were too, her disabled arm was a vicious weapon to friend and foe alike.

How we all hated Sunday afternoon visiting. Even though all the fruit, sweets, cakes, biscuits and crisps were supposed to be handed in to the ward office, only a token amount ever got there, the rest was stuffed non-stop into their offspring by the parents, with the consequent results for us to deal with after they had gone. It was a revelation to me that some food looked the same in a vomit bowl as it had before being swallowed. One boy had eaten the little blue packet of salt along with his crisps; it was returned unopened!

On the whole I was enjoying nursing but was not entirely sure that it was to be my life's work. Pay was £1 14s 8d per month, with board, lodging, laundry and uniform provided, but it seemed a long way ahead before I ever saw any more.

My eldest brother, who was teaching in a town nearby, was sounding out the possibility of teaching abroad and there might be a place for me too. In the meantime I carried on with my training.

One ward was to be used as an experimental one under an Australian nursing sister – Sister Elizabeth Kenny, who had revolutionary ideas about nursing the victims of polio-myelitis, previously known as infantile paralysis. This term was incorrect as any age group could contract the disease.

Children from all over Europe and Britain came to see her, some very rich indeed, others very poor, but all with varying degrees of paralysis. I was chosen to be on this ward and the pace was hectic. We were caught between our own staff, medical and nursing, with their rules, and the Australian contingent with their very different outlook. It was a constant charging up and down the ward, carrying patients of all weights and sizes, until we were exhausted but muscular. Baths and exercising of flaccid muscles were the treatment; this had worked in Australia at the beginning of the infection, in a very different climate from this cold, northern hemisphere. All the children had been paralysed for years and their muscles were beyond recall, so the experiment was deemed very useful, but unhelpful to any but those in the early stages where muscles could be saved. So the children all went home again and we'd developed muscles worthy of weightlifters, lost weight, and were fit, though tired. Never in my wildest dreams did I think I'd nurse patients in the acute stages of polio, watch them recover, or die, nor know that I would go to Australia twice.

My brother now had a post lined up for a school in the Nilgiri Hills in South India. There was a vacancy too for a school matron in one of the girls' boarding houses. This appealed to me, and my interview took place on Victoria Station, of all places. The interviewer was very sedate, long-haired and a very Evangelical Christian. My hair was short, my faith nowhere near her standard, but she decided that I had qualities yet to be developed, so the job was mine if I wanted. I did.

Going back to the hospital to resign gave me a few uneasy moments and I knew that in breaking my contract I'd have to pay the LCC compensation. Fortunately this was my brother's responsibility.

To my surprise the matron asked me to reconsider my decision. She said that all the sisters under whom I'd worked that year spoke highly of how I was shaping and that eventually I would make a good nurse; that was why I'd been chosen for the polio ward. All this was news to me. No-one had given any of us much encouragement since we'd started, though others had fared less happily than I, and we all put it down to normal training.

My mind was made up so off to County Hall I went, by Westminster Bridge, to see the Matron in Chief, and pay my contract-breaking fine. There I had my first experience of a lift which shot me up bodily several storeys, but left my stomach behind on the ground floor! The matron was a most human woman who realised there was no point in trying to make me think again, so I paid up and left. Once again it was not part of any notion I had then that in years to come I would start nursing again and follow it through to the end.

2

India

War clouds were gathering as we sailed for India in 1939, but we saw no reason to stay. After all, things had looked equally black the year before, and war had been averted then, so why not now? I think we both knew that such an opportunity would not come again. There was too much of interest for homesickness to take over as we left unromantic Tilbury. The Bay of Biscay and Gulf of Lyons weeded out the poor sailors from the rest; neither of us turned a hair and we enjoyed our meals.

Going ashore at various ports we enchantment for me, as were all the new smells, unsanitary and foul, no doubt, but different, that's what counted. The Suez Canal, with

Bedouin encampments, kept me out of my cabin until we were through.

Life on an ocean-going liner was utterly different from anything I'd imagined. Class distinction was there in a big way. I'd seen this in school among some staff towards 'scholarship girls'. This included me, but as my real friends were all fee-paying and loyal, I wasn't affected. Others had less fortunate lives; the fact that brains had got us there didn't count. The differences between passengers was most marked. Indian civil servants, army officers and their respective families were socially far superior to clergy, missionaries and the rest. The stewards left no-one in any doubt as to who counted! We didn't belong to any faction, so were just accepted as unclassified persons going out east.

Bombay was fascinating but bewildering. We were met by the head of General Motors in India and taken to his lovely home until we took off for Madras late in the evening. A feeling of complete detachment from real life came over me as the heat of Bombay pavements rose up and hit me. Not for a moment though did I regret being there. We watched coolies load our trunks, last seen being put in a railway van at home. Our hand luggage came with us in the kind man's car, the sort I'd never expected to ride in.

The coolness indoors was soothing, but the soft-footed servants were quite unnerving. I'd never been waited on at table in a home before, so I was scared of doing the wrong thing. Our host soon put us at ease and gave us some very sound advice about life in this new country. Corn on the cob was another strange new thing, now an everyday food. I began to wonder what I'd let myself in for.

We were taken on a sightseeing tour of the city, seeing lepers for the first time, and such poverty that it was very disturbing. Whatever we'd expected it wasn't this.

Victoria Station was nothing like its London counterpart. Everywhere there was seething humanity, pushing each other around to find a flat surface on which to sit or lie, shrouded in very off-white material. Many looked dead, stretched out immobile on the platforms but springing to life when the shrieking train came in. They hung onto the outside, they pushed through open windows, anywhere to get a toe- or finger-hold before the train started.

No-one had prepared us for what we should need for a night on an Indian train. We had been mystified by the canvas rolls carried on the top of the luggage piles until we watched our travelling companion unroll his. There was a fully made-up bed, minus mattress of course, which, spread on the bunk, made a cosy place for the night's sleep. I had a travelling rug, but all our bedding was in our trunks. The Indian gentleman was most charming and perturbed that nobody had advised us about our travelling requirements, so he gave me one of his pillows and two blankets, while my poor brother had to make do with the meagre comfort of my rug, his coat and our rolled-up towels for a pillow.

It was hard to settle for the night because our companion was so interesting and informative. He showed us the intricacies of the little washroom with its peculiar lavatory, a hole in the floor with wooden treads for feet on either side, and how the upper berth let down for the third bed. What greenhorns we were, but not for long – we learned quickly.

The rhythm of the train was pretty constant until slowing down to enter a station, so sleep was shallow until tiredness took over. At Madras we said goodbye to our travelling companion and were met by another stranger, equally kind. At least we were halfway to our journey's end.

Again there was a lack of flushing toilet facilities. In the Bombay house things had been 'normal' but here there were commodes, known as thunderboxes, one per person. After using it one had to leave the outer door ajar for the lowliest-caste servant, a sweeper of either sex, to take and empty it, then replace it. A bath – bliss even in an old-fashioned zinc tub – then a real English breakfast, followed by deep restorative sleep, was the order of the day. I awoke to hear 'Green pigs, missie ma, green pigs' outside the window. Were the pigs different in colour in this strange land? All I could see as I looked out was a slim Indian girl with a basket on her head, calling out 'Green pigs'. I'd not known that the p's and f's were interchangeable and that it was lovely fresh figs she was selling.

There was time to be taken around Madras before we set off for Ootacamund, and it was strange to see old, familiar names of food, but in new packaging, like Anchor butter, and Cadbury products, all in sealed tins. We saw lepers again, very disfigured, beggars, maimed folk and pot-bellied children, as well as happy, healthy-looking ones. I'd yet to realise what a land of contrasts we had come to. Then, back to the railway station to catch the mainline train to the junction where we would have to change and get the last train on our journey, a wheel and cog one up to the hills. This time we were better prepared for the night. We had a little coupé to ourselves, and knew that we must not sleep too soundly and miss our connection. We didn't and were soon climbing through wonderful scenery in the early morning, to go up to over 7,000 feet above sea level. Huge gorges fell away on one side, towering cliffs were on the other, a road with incredible hairpin bends kept coming into view and then going again. New trees and birds were everywhere, the sun getting higher all the time. We marvelled at the engineering skills that had built this railway. It was a relief to get to the school, unpack, settle in and see again the familiar photos and possessions.

Ooty was a hill station to which the plains dwellers who could afford it came to escape the intense summer heat, so we had a social whirl for part of the year and quietness for the rest. The hills were like our South

Downs, larks singing overhead as they did at home, and in the winter we had sparkling frosts, night and morning, and lovely log fires at night.

To me, Ooty will always be a place of enchantment; there I first saw and smelled eucalyptus trees. There, arum lilies, so beloved of Easter brides, grew like weeds around the school playing fields, and camellias were an everyday sight. In the downland turf and grasses we found wild orchids growing near unfamiliar wild guava bushes. There on our walks, we saw the ancient tribe of Todas, the men incredibly handsome, tending their cattle near their primitive homes. My home seemed on another planet, and because by now the European war had started, unreal.

I was happy in the school until the headmaster's wife died and the school was taken over by a bigoted, narrow-minded couple, who caused great distress and unhappiness to most of the staff. The war was beginning to impinge on us too; mail was held up for ages, British goods were unavailable, and some goods were in short supply. My brother went into the Indian Army and I, with a friend, went up to schools in Mussoorie in the Himalayas. Details of my life in India have no relevance except that they helped in forming the person I eventually became.

I was sitting up in a hospital bed, recovering from appendicitis, when a grey-haired woman came into the ward to see a girl whose home was in Gaya, miles away. Mother had spoken of several people she knew in India, including one from a well-known local family who had taught with my aunt, but I'd not met her. Passing my bed she looked and said, 'Are you Hope Gravett?' When I said that I was, she said that I was so much like my mother when she was young as to be unmistakeable. That brought the tears, which until then had never been a threat, and I longed to see the rest of my family. It was no good brooding though, and that encounter meant that I had a home to go to for holidays and Christmas.

I joined the Army YMCA, for I had to do something in war service, and ran a canteen and cinema in Bengal. War with Japan had started, meaning more to us than the one back home. I saw many of the 14th Army, and in one place, for a short time, had a Chindit assault course nearby. For the first time in my life I met huge men from Africa with the West African Rifles. They were always cheerful and smiling, and could eat such quantities of steak, eggs and chips as to leave me speechless. I also met Australians, Americans and hundreds of my own compatriots.

My brother and I met as often as possible; I managed to get to his wedding, but travel was not easy. Vast numbers of troops were on the move at a time when there was constant unrest among the Indian Congress supporters of Mahatma Gandhi. At times the railway tracks were torn up, leaving hundreds at the mercy of hotheads, often stranded miles from anywhere. Eventually, with experience I'd never imagined would be mine, with India poised for the greatest unrest and bloodshed since the Mutiny, I sailed for home unwillingly, a very different person from the one who'd left five and a half years before.

3

Back Home Again

The war in Europe was nearing the end when I docked at Liverpool one grey November night. We'd passed wrecks in the Mersey with their red warning lights that made this war seem a bit more real to me, who had never been in an air raid or heard gunfire except in practice for when the Japanese came.

There was nothing to commend England to me – cold, grey and drizzling – in a city I'd only heard of. The money was strange and even the thought of seeing home and parents again couldn't compensate for the feeling of utter dejection that threatened to overwhelm me. Why had I left warm, sunny skies to come back to this unfriendly, unwelcoming place? I wallowed in self-pity, not willing to admit that no-one had compelled me to return. It had merely been the constant suggestions on my father's part that he was worried about my mother's health, and that we all knew the writing was on the wall for the British in India, but were loath to acknowledge it. My faithful bedding roll was no use in that cold, crowded train, as full as an Indian one, but without the jollity and life force I'd got used to. I couldn't realise just how hard life had been here through the war years and how tired everyone was. There were no sellers of fruit, hot snacks and tea, no colourful saris to enliven the journey, it was all grey and boring. I'd forgotten too that people didn't talk to one another on English trains, it was like being a stranger in my own land. When we slowed down and stopped, for no apparent reason, I wondered aloud if there was a cow on the line – trains were always having to stop for this in India. The horrified looks of the other passengers made me aware of how mad it must have sounded; I'm sure they thought I had got away from somewhere for the insane!

Memory fails me as to how I got all my baggage across London to Victoria, perversely longing for its namesake in Bombay. The southern electric train was warmer and more familiar than the one from Liverpool had been, and the sight of the South Downs roused me a little so that I got apprehensive about seeing home and parents again. All the houses and gardens by the side of the railway seemed so small after the vastness of India. Hundreds of poor Indians had lived in hovels, the less poor in better houses, and the rich in huge, lovely estates, or city houses, but they all had sunshine, which seemed to be lacking here at home. Just then a weak glimmer of winter sunshine tried to break through the grey clouds, and I saw how green everything was, even in winter, so my spirits rose a little. Of course there were no coolies at my home station, my parents had no idea that I was so close to them, but there was an outside porter, a useful breed no longer seen, who would trundle your luggage on a trolley to your home if it wasn't too far away. Mine wasn't and a man who had known me all my life told me to get along home and leave the rest to him. England became real to me then – I could leave my belongings safely with this man, not just because he knew me, whereas in India we'd had to keep our eye on any carriers in case they went in the wrong direction.

As I saw my home again I began to get cold feet once more – did I walk in, or did I knock at the door? How silly one can get with tiredness, coldness and hunger! Of course I needn't knock on the door of my own home, so I turned the handle and called out 'Mother', as I'd always done, knowing that if she didn't answer, my world would fall apart; she'd always been there without fail, and this day was no different. She seemed so small and tired, but still my mother, then my father appeared, so I knew

34

I was home.

Not that I settled easily; I would have done anything to get away from the sheer greyness and cold that surrounded me. I knew I'd never get back to India, but knew too that I could not bear to live at home again – I had to get a job that would let me get home for the holidays, but no more. It was hard getting to know the family, the land, and myself again; I must have been very hard to tolerate then.

For a few months I worked in the Army YMCA in the old Westminster Hospital, then went to Cornwall as a school matron until I had to go home for a while as my mother was ill and needed surgery. As soon as she'd recovered I went to be in charge of the sick bay at the junior school of the Royal Merchant Navy. Most of the children had lost their fathers in the war and they came from all sorts of backgrounds. The headmaster was an old Indian hand, and we used to talk about it to each other and the children. Talking about it gradually dissolved the lump of misery that had been with me all the time since my return – it was always under the surface, very insistent sometimes, so I was glad to realise that I'd got it out of my system at last.

I was jolted out of my new-found contentment by the sudden death of my father, emotionally devastating, and I knew that in fairness to my sister, years my junior, I would have to go home. Regretfully I gave in my resignation, finished the term out, and that was another part of my life finished. I didn't know that the next bit was to prove the last part of my working life, or that it held so much for me.

4

Nursing – Second Time Round

In the local paper they were advertising a two-year course of nurse training for State Enrolment – one year of lectures and ward experience, then a written and practical exam, followed by a year of further nursing, before being put on the National Roll and getting a badge and certificate.

Four hospitals were involved in the scheme: a local infection one, which was the parent hospital, a children's heart home a few miles along the coast, a post-operative one on the edge of a ducal estate, and a small GP-run hospital which did a fair amount of routine surgery, thus giving a good selection of basic types of nursing.

I applied, was interviewed and accepted,

and started on a life which has given me more than I ever hoped for in job satisfaction, fulfilment, pleasure, sorrow, all jumbled up together, but when I started I had none of these thoughts.

Being told to report for uniform fitting two days before the fateful starting date, I cycled from home on a trial run to see how long it would take. Uphill most of the way meant I was warm and slightly puffed by the time I arrived. I was handed a thick mauve and white dress to try on, so unyielding in its texture that when the numerous buttons were fastened I was in a straitjacket and could scarcely breathe, let alone move!

'How's that?' asked the home sister.

'It depends upon what you want me to do in it,' I replied. Such a surprised look came over her face. Who was I to question her choice of uniform size? Her mouth opened to say something which never got said, for on closer inspection she could see my breathing was being obstructed by the tight bodice and neck. So, grudgingly, she had to concede that it was a little too tight – her words, not mine. To her regret, only new frocks would fit me. In my innocence, I'd not thought of being given cast-offs. So three new frocks were mine, like mattress ticking – very durable – hot in the summer and uncomfortable all the year round. The sleeves were too short for my long arms, but I was told that starched cuffs would hide that deficiency. In a measure they did but without comfort. Caps, cuffs, aprons and collars were given, with strict instructions never to lend anything to anyone, and I was launched for the second time into the world of nursing. The collars were starched to a knife-edge finish, and only when one got soiled and needed changing was my neck free from a raw, red band. The studs used for fixing collar to dress were so hard to get through the starched layers, I had to leave home ten minutes early when it was collar-changing time.

The first four weeks were spent in school, where from the depths of my memory I dredged up all sorts of useful knowledge from my first effort. Then we were all sent to a ward either in the parent hospital, or in one of the others. I was told to report to a ward at the top of the hill on which the hospital was built, where there were 12 men, mostly young, with TB.

The staff nurse told me to go along the veranda and say hello to all the men in five double and two single cubicles. Stiffly starched and rustling I creaked along. In one cubicle two young men were lying reading. They looked up when I dutifully said 'Hello' and one said, 'Hello, you won't do for this ward, you're the wrong shape.' This seemed a very strange greeting.

The second one tried to explain. 'You'll soon see when the sister comes, you are too tall and your bosom's too high, not big enough to rest on the stable doors.' Still taken aback, I looked at the doors and found that they were indeed stable type, four parts which could be opened or shut independently, but until I saw the sister comfortably resting her ample bosom on the lower half, I couldn't see what my shape had to do with it. I had a job not to laugh and cut off my training before it had really begun.

I soon settled into the life of this ward, where the apparent good health of most of the 12 was very deceptive. Long periods of rest were related to the results of X-rays, sputum and blood tests, and the very trying test of washing out stomach juices of those who had no sputum. The elation of those who were allowed to stay up for longer periods was tempered by the frustration of those whose hours were unchanged or shortened. These young men were full of hope and high spirits, which had to be curbed to save their physical energy. It seemed very hard to have to subdue their natural exuberance, even though it was essential. Some of the drugs they had to swallow, day after day, were unpalatable and nauseating, and the food was deadly dull, but nutritious. Indigestion from drugs and food gave more distress than the disease itself.

For bed-making we had to wear long gowns and masks. These brought all sorts of remarks about sheiks and their harems, all very childish but hurting no-one. It made the boys feel they were chatting up the girls. We were warned not to get familiar with any patient, or let them get fresh with us. As for a kiss, however chaste – unthinkable! Dressed in stiff mattress-ticking frocks, buttoned from neck to wrists, with an all-enveloping gown and face mask added, it was hard to think that the men saw us as women, let alone get amorous! But, let no-one underestimate the ability of men and women to light a spark between them in the most unlikely situations. A man would have to be very far gone not to respond to a pair of sparkling eyes above a face mask, and many a temporary romance sprang up, in spite of dire warnings. Two of our year did pick up the infection, but as far as we knew were no more emotionally responsive than the rest; besides, where was the opportunity?

Night duty on this ward was very lonely, with sinister rustlings and creaks from the trees outside, and bed creakings and snoring from inside. Some of the lighter sleepers got fed up with the others' snores and would ask us to think of ways to stop it. I never could.

The night was spent in the ward kitchen-cum-office, in the middle of the cubicles, with a ventilator window high up, on a level with the hillside at the back, and mice used to squeeze through onto the cupboard top below. I dreaded them coming down to floor level. One night, wrapped in my cloak, far too cold to feel even vaguely sleepy, I heard a squeak. There was a large mouse with his beady eyes on me! It was useless to yell for help so I seized a flit spray gun, one of the old pre-aerosol types, and gave him a quick burst. He sneezed repeatedly, wiping his eyes with his little paws, and looked so pathetic I felt very guilty until he reeled drunkenly over the edge! I shot out into the cold night air, leaving him to find his way out too. I didn't see him again, but never was the morning light more welcome.

My allotted time on this ward came to an end, so with yet another chest X-ray to see I'd picked up nothing by misfortune or misbehaviour, I was sent on my way.

My next patients were mainly children, with whooping cough, scarlet fever, food poisoning, or dysentery, with an occasional adult with typhoid picked up from abroad. The summer was a very hot one, before the discovery of the Salk vaccine against polio, so in no time we were nursing very ill patients of all age groups. It was unbelievable that we were to see children die, or become permanently disabled, and quite frightening to see those of our own age groups in the same dire straits.

Sister Kenny and her revolutionary methods came back to me as the old way of treatment was used: good and affected muscles alike were kept immobilised by sandbags, with no passive exercises. I kept wondering whether it wouldn't hurt to try a new form of care. After all, what was there to lose? The conventional way left irreparable damage, the new might not in the early stages, it had worked in Australia; so why not here in the summer heat? But I was only there to do as I was bidden, not question medical decisions, and so I said nothing of my previous experience. One little girl, with all her limbs affected, kept asking when could she walk home to Mummy. In between asking she would sing, 'How much is the doggie in the window?' over and over again. In the next cubicle was a young man, with children of his own. One side was completely paralysed and the other partially. His anguish was mental as well as physical, for nobody could tell if he would ever walk again, yet he hated to be so dependent on us for everything. He was so patient with the little girl he could only hear. Their voices comforted each other and he painstakingly sang all the words of her song until she learned them too. Another small boy, very paralysed, spoke wistfully of when he'd played football and could we please tell him when he could play again. These three and all who recovered were sent to Stanmore Orthopaedic Hospital in Middlesex, eventually walking again with limps, supports, and special footwear to hold the weak and useless muscles.

We nursed several young women, two of whom were married and very worried about their families, but their courage was never in doubt, they were determined to recover and go home to run their homes as before. Another, in the early part of pregnancy, was convinced that her baby would be born normally, at full term, and that once she had a pram to push she'd be walking again. This buoyed her up in the most trying, painful times. We heard that she did indeed have her baby normally and that walking came in the end.

A girl in her late teens was very affected by the disease, even part of her face, but never once did she think that she wouldn't recover. When warned that without callipers she'd be unable to walk, she just laughed and said that on her day of discharge from Stanmore, she'd run down the ward, without any supports, and she did, proving what will-power, hope and good physiotherapy could do.

The most frightening type of polio was the bulbar type, in which the soft palate was paralysed, and breathing and swallowing were impaired, sometimes stopping altogether. Saliva couldn't be swallowed and had to be sucked out to prevent lungs being filled with fluid instead of air. How could one allay the fears of a child who didn't know what was happening and an adult who knew only too well? We grew to know the meaning of a slightly nasal change in the tone of voice, and the convulsive, useless attempts to swallow. We seemed to have such small means of help at our disposal, only care; even this was hard when helplessness and hopelessness seemed all around us. It was no use asking why a boy of nine should die, while a girl, a little older, equally ill with bulbar polio, should live. We could only feel sorrow for one family and joy for the other.

A man in his thirties was severely paralysed, even his diaphragm was affected, so an iron lung was to be used in a last bid for life. It was most harrowing to hear him protest, with failing breath, that we were putting him in his coffin before he was dead. We felt every failing breath and protest personally. We didn't mind the hard work, but it did hurt to see children suffer, and some die. It was just as painful and frightening when it happened to adults. Three nurses were detailed to nurse the man in the lung – speed was essential when nursing procedures meant that he had to be out of the lung for even a short time. I was one of the three, only leaving him for meals and off-duty breaks, which we had to have to be able to carry on. For a short while it seemed as though death was going to lose out, so it was a shock to find that he'd died when I was off duty, and such a bitter tragedy for his wife and family.

However, there were bright moments among the gloom. It was great to hear voices coming back to normal and muscles beginning to recover, so that dates could be set for a transfer to Stanmore to finish what we had started. The youngest patient was a baby boy, ten months old, with one leg paralysed. He was a safety valve for us all, especially for the young nurses. A great fuss could be made of a baby, and who could see the tears while a baby was being hugged? He helped us through the utter misery of that time.

One young girl had lain unconscious and paralysed for several days and her recovery very doubtful. Two of us were blanket-bathing her and I tickled the sole of one foot – it twitched! Neither of us could believe our eyes so we called the sister in. I did the same thing again, saying, 'Are you ticklish, Judy?' The toes moved again and after what seemed an eternity of waiting, she nodded her head and whispered, 'Yes.' We were filled with disproportionate joy, for it was to take a long time for there to be any more visible progress, but it was a vital start.

The summer heat subsided and so did the polio epidemic; very few people on the outside were aware of the numbers affected, or the deaths. It was best that way and we were only too glad to put it behind us.

There must be nobody who has not heard of lockjaw – the very name can strike terror in one's mind. With no more polio patients coming in, we had time to think of happier things than death and deformities, so we were less tired and overwrought when a man was admitted with tetanus (lockjaw). In spite of pumping him full of anti-tetanus serum, his condition was hopeless from the start. He'd scratched himself while working in his well-manured garden.

Everything had to be done to keep him calm and comfortable in a darkened room so that the light could not hurt his eyes. No sudden noise, jolt or abrupt movement was allowed, as all these things could bring on sudden, devastating convulsions. Helping to nurse him made me realise something had been happening to me; I was happy. Nursing wasn't any more just a way of earning my living, this was my life as I wanted it, the first time I'd ever been sure. I don't mean I became a perfect nurse overnight, or at any time, but I was intent on finishing my training and getting a job as an enrolled nurse locally. If anyone had suggest that I, of my own free will, would start yet another course of training to go a stage further, I'd have told them they were crazy.

With cases of whooping cough, scarlet fever, and a girl very ill with typhoid, life at night was non-stop rounds, racing from one cubicle to another as everybody seemed to be choking or coughing at the same time. Each cubicle had its own gown and mask for the nurses' use, so it was out of one and into the next, with hand-washing before and after every change. We had no cross infection so we must have done the rituals properly.

At one of the busiest times we had no

night sister, so a staff nurse was put on the TB block, and I on the assorted infections cubicle ward. The powers that be decided that I could keep my head in any emergency and would call the staff nurse if worried. The matron did a late night round, then left, arranging that the staff nurse would come at midnight to help me with the injections. One very bright, moonlit night, we'd done the injections and had a cup of coffee together. This was allowed, and I went to the door, remaining in earshot, to see my colleague on her way. She was Irish, of great wit and fiery temper, so when loud snores greeted us in the open air she clutched my arm saying, 'Merciful Mother of God, what's that?' Before I could say a word, she rushed back into the ward and came out brandishing a large, hooked stick we used for fishing the bedpans out of the steriliser. Sounding and looking very ferocious, she shouted, 'Come out, you wicked old tramp, you should be ashamed frightening two poor nurses in the middle of the night!' Of course no-one answered; it was only two large hedgehogs under the hedge. I'd never have believed that they snorted like that, and wondered what a tramp would have made of a stick-wielding nurse.

When the night sister came back I was sent on my way again.

The next place was the children's heart home, where my new-found contentment was interrupted, not shattered. The patients were mainly from London or the Midlands, with various heart troubles. No surgery was done here, London or Birmingham took care of that when the time came. Very few parents could afford to visit, so it was a battle to keep them amused under strict routine. They could be little terrors and many of the young nurses had their spirits almost broken by this and the attitude of the senior staff. We trainees were treated as glorified nursemaids, housemaids and deputy cooks, doing all the cleaning and work, when there were no domestic staff on duty. We had all the shoes to clean and were cheap, captive labour. The seniors were a law unto themselves and so long as they weren't bothered they didn't mind what went on. Reading aloud, whilst the children were lying on their beds, took hours of each day but at least we had a sit-down! The non-fluent readers had their lives made hell by some of the biggest boys who should never have been put in with younger ones. Luckily I could read and make myself heard, but anyone who couldn't hold the children's attention had to cope with them getting up, shouting and fighting, then the scathing sarcasm of the seniors who never had to cope with any of it.

Having to get up at 5.30 a.m. to catch a train that would get me there in time to cook the junior staff's breakfasts and take early tea to the matron and her deputy soon palled. If it had been vital for the health of the children, I would have accepted it as part of training, but this had nothing to do with it. Not being a teenager, and certainly not in awe of the seniors, I went to the matron of the parent hospital, really our boss, and put her in the picture. I'm sure others had complained, but her surprise was all that a good actress's should be. My forcefulness or something made her do what should have been done before. Duties were well-defined, domestic chores were out and no nurse spent so long there as before. My protests were on behalf of the others as well as for me.

On Sunday mornings we had to take the children to the parish church, two to each canvas and metal invalid chair. The big child had the smaller on his/her lap. Most of the chairs were past their best, and if we were at all delayed in getting off, the worst chairs were left. One Sunday the worst of all was left for me, it had a sideways bias and no matter how one wrenched the wretched thing, with two children on board, it was impossible to keep straight. A sister, also late, kept asking querulously why I kept going off the kerb. At one stage, to my passengers' delight, I was heading straight towards the local cinema on the opposite side of the road! The sister's comments were no help. I wanted to tell her to push it herself if she could do better, but settled for saying that if I could keep it straight, I would. By almost dislocating my wrists and the chair's joints, we got to the church as the choir was filing in. Afterwards I whisked my two out smartish, and got a good chair, with no guilty feelings about leaving the demon behind for someone else. But when I saw that the most slightly built of us was grappling with the demon to try to get back on time for lunch, I dumped my two and went back to help her. The most annoying aspect was the senior staff's inability to appreciate how antiquated, badly maintained and downright dangerous most of the chairs were. So long as no child fell out and the chairs hung together, that was all that mattered. Still, that Sunday finished off the demon chair forever, and my time was finished too. I wasn't sorry.

Autumn passed and my next place was at a post-operative hospital on the edge of the Duke of Norfolk's estate, with lovely grounds to enjoy. There was a nucleus of long-stay patients as well as post-surgery ones. There were two main wards and four single rooms. Wide verandas from both wards gave splendid vantage points for birdwatching. Cock pheasants with harems strutted up to be fed, and several tits, thrushes and blackbirds became very friendly. The patients used to save all sorts of titbits for their birds and gained enormous pleasure from watching their antics. The grey squirrels that cause so much damage to woodlands made everyone laugh at their antics. In the right season woodpeckers could be heard drilling in the trees and occasionally flew by showing their marvellous colours. Nightingales too were close by; it was a very tranquil spot to either die or recover in.

My first Christmas was spent here with old-fashioned celebrations, refreshing after the high drama of the summer and its polio. One ward was cleared, and the women who were left were put into the four small rooms, while the men stayed put. The empty ward was used as a day room for all the patients. It stayed that way until after the New Year. Decorations were put up. Large logs were brought in so that a gorgeous open fire burned every day. Only minimal work was done, and no-one was really ill, so they could enjoy all the food and festivities.

A surgeon came from the general hospital nearest to us and carved the turkey. Members of the ducal family came on Christmas Day – their turkey was saved for New Year celebrations. It was all very unhurried and nostalgic. I should soon have tired of that sort of nursing – there was no challenge, and nothing to keep abreast of in the field of new drugs, treatment etc. – but it did me good, mentally and physically, after the trauma of polio.

The birds had rich pickings from all the nuts, fats and leftovers, and in the sheltered woodland hollows we found primroses, blooming weeks ahead of any elsewhere, giving promise of spring to come.

On that Christmas Day there were no buses and few trains so I took my bike on the train to the nearest station, ready to cycle the ten miles or so back home at the end of my duty. Naturally it was dark at 4.30 p.m. when I got out of my uniform and started for home. The road was through a lot of woodland, much of it uphill, so on one steep hill I got off and pushed my bike. No other living soul was abroad, I felt as if I was the only one left alive, when an unearthly, hollow, echoing noise got me on my bike again. My jelly-like legs acted as unwilling pistons to keep the pedals flying round. It was only a poor, solitary cow, with her head over the gate, voicing her indigestion to anything within earshot. Home was reached in record time. I'd have won that stage in the Round Britain Milk Race easily! I was glowing with warmth at the end, quite ready for the family meal, even though I'd had a good one midday.

Night duty here seemed to make the rest of the world very remote. Two of us were on duty, with trained staff on call. A policeman came in the early hours each night to see that all was well; this was most comforting. At each end of the upstairs was a fire escape and they also got checked to see that no-one could get in. One night the front doorbell rang in the middle of the night but when we got there no-one could be seen. Then the back doorbell rang – again, nobody was there. Going together made us feel a bit braver than going alone, but by the time the invisible being had rung both bells for about ten minutes, we were nearly gibbering with fright. The fervour and warmth of our welcome took the policeman by surprise. He'd not expected that at 2 a.m.! We told him about the invisible bell-ringer, so he did a thorough check, and the girl on duty with me insisted that he looked in the mortuary to see that the body in there had not come alive again! He found large footprints going up and down the fire escapes and across the grass, but we never did find out who scared us so.

Soon it was time for me to move again.

My next place was at the small GP hospital in another seaside town just along the coast. I had to go by train and then walk. The matron was very good and I usually worked a straight shift from the early morning till 4.30 p.m. There was no high-powered surgery here, but all the patients were persons, not a case study or number.

In no time I was back on night duty, with a very unapproachable Scots sister, hyper-efficient, who tended to regard any one not doing a full SRN course as a lesser being. Still, we managed to get on all right. She taught me a lot, and as she was one of the old school who had been taught never to unbend with a junior, we did surprisingly well. She once grudgingly conceded that I had common sense and in time should make a good nurse. High praise indeed! I had to do alternate weekends on night duty; when the sister was off I had another trainee with me, with trained staff on call. I enjoyed the extra responsibility, though life seemed a constant rush, on and off trains, and in and out of uniform which still hadn't softened after months of wear. One night, undressing as I dashed through the front door, I was met by one of the day staff, who told me to hurry into the theatre where there was an emergency 'with all his insides out on his tummy, like sausages, only longer'. What choice clinical details to give me on my first visit to theatre! Imagine then my feelings at midnight when I opened the fridge door to see what had been left for our meal and found raw, pallid sausages! It was a very long time before I could think of a sausage without revulsion.

A bottle of Lucozade was used as a potent weapon one morning by a woman who went berserk suddenly. She shook it hard, building up the pressure, and perched herself on the bedhead, spraying anyone who came near her. Shrieking, 'I'll tell the mayor and his corporation about all of you,' she threw the bottle onto the floor, where it smashed into dozens of pieces, then quick as a flash got the next bottle out of her locker. We had to do something before the day staff came on duty, but what? We decided that if we approached from both sides she could only keep her eye on one of us. The stickiness underfoot was awful, and so was all the glass, our uniforms were getting sprayed too. Our approaches confused her, as we'd hoped, so with one looking to see there were no further supplies, the other wrested the bottle from her. She had surprising strength as we tried to clean her and her bed up. The mayor was constantly being called on to help save her, and we had to leave her on a pile of sticky bedding, beyond any co-operation. Sometime during the day she was transferred to the local mental hospital.

5

A Qualified Success

All through these months spent at the various hospitals we had all gone back to the parent hospital for lectures each week. We'd enjoyed catching up with the news from the others of the same group, but now it was time for the two exams. The practical one was to show the various nursing things we'd learned, like bandaging, bed-bathing and anything we'd been shown. The examiner, a visiting sister tutor, fired questions at us as we worked. I enjoyed that exam very much but the written was an insult to normal intelligence. No-one has ever told me to which branch of nursing the question, 'What would you do with an empty sardine tin?' belonged. I said I'd put it in the bin, only to be told afterwards that the proper answer should have been, burn the tin to remove the oil, then wrap in paper and put in the bin. Another bit of education I'd not known was lacking before! The other two questions had some vague nursing connection but were just as futile. As I passed both sections, my answer to the fishy question couldn't have been vital. After that it was into my second year except that I had no part in the summer carbon copy of polio – others had to cope with the misery and deaths – neither did I have a repeat visit to the heart hospital.

It was back to the little country hospital for Christmas, but the patients were less fit than last time, so they couldn't really enjoy things. Soon after Christmas the snow started falling heavily throughout one afternoon, so I was told to get off home. Having my bike with me, I started to ride very gingerly down the road to the nearest station, in the ruts made by cars. The snow's whiteness in the late-afternoon gloom gave an eerie light, but the dynamo on my back wheel soon got too clogged to work. I had a hand torch in the front and hoped that any motorist would pick up my red reflector in the headlights. I need not have worried, no-one else was daft enough to be out in the weather like that. With snow on my face and my eyebrows encrusted, I saw the station lights ahead, and thankfully fell off my bike when I got there. A mug of tea by the porter's fire soon thawed me out as I waited for the train. (Years later, in another hospital the porter regaled the rest of the ward with my epic ride.) The roads were too glassy to ride on when I reached my home station so I slipped and slithered along, with the bike always going in the opposite direction from my feet. I didn't give a thought to the morning as I got into my warm bed.

When my alarm went off it was a real struggle to get out of bed, but it didn't occur to me to stay home. So I duly slithered and slid, minus bike, off to the station, with the prospect of a long walk ahead at the other end as no buses were on such icy roads. What a walk it was! I could have done with snowshoes or penguin feet, but had to make do with a pair of wellies, arriving late on duty for the first time. Everyone was so surprised to see me at all that I was given a cup of hot Bovril before starting work. During the day I was told that I was going back on night duty, so I would have four nights off before doing ten on. Later on I did slither to the station and home, feeling as though I'd been doing it all my life, and my muscles endorsing that feeling! By the time I had to go back the snow had gone, so my journeys were uneventful.

The nightingales sang very early that spring, just before my two years were up, pouring out their song for hours at night. I had a cockney girl on night duty with me, full of fun with a caustic wit and very decided views of likes and dislikes. The birds' song annoyed her so much that she kept on moaning. 'I wish those b– birds would shut up, they're getting on my nerves.'

In the end I too wished they'd be quiet, just to shut her up.

I said goodbye to this happy little place and to the parent one, only going back there to collect my badge and certificate. As far as I knew then, it was the end of training. I'd done what I'd set out to do, and had a job lined up with the GP hospital. I had the same uncomfortable uniform, but with a new belt with my new status. Thus equipped, I started on what I thought was to be a permanent post, an end to study and training. How wrong I was only became clear as the months went by.

Strangely enough there seemed to be little difference in being a trained as opposed to trainee nurse. The matron had always encouraged me to take any responsibility offered, and after a year I realised that I should like to have these responsibilities as a right, not by favour, but I got on with the work and stifled my thoughts. I still did the weekend relief for the Scots sister at times, but it was worked out fairly so that all had some part of the weekend off duty. Many times I had to assist in theatre, taking it for granted that I was capable of doing all that was asked of me.

During the summer we were very busy in Casualty. Holidaymakers caught their fingers in deckchairs, roasted themselves alive in the sun, scorched with salt-laden breezes; at time fish-hooks got caught under the skin, making the removal very painful. One night, just as we'd finished settling the patients the back doorbell rang. Outside there were two men, one holding his ear. They were Australians on a European tour with their girlfriends. 'No funny business, you understand,' as if anything they did was any of my concern! They had tents but tried to get the girls a caravan when possible. This night, they were going down the caravan steps when a moth, attracted by the light, swooped and went into one man's ear, where it still was, driving him crazy with its fluttering. It sounded rather far-fetched but they were steady on their feet and no alcoholic fumes were around, so I got an instrument with a light, to look in his ear. Sure enough there was the moth, in such a confined space no wonder he was tormented. I filled an ear syringe with warm water and gave a gentle squirt into the ear. Out flew the moth, shook its wings and went off, much to the men's dismay. They wailed that the girls would never believe it. That was soon remedied as there were so many moths circling the outside light that we caught one easily, put it into an empty matchbox, and sent two very satisfied customers on their way.

On another occasion, sounds of maudlin, drunken laughter greeted us just before midnight, and a voice loudly protesting that he didn't want to be brought to this b– place, followed by a thud against the front door. We both rushed to see and found a Fleet Air Arm man lurching around with an ashen face. A companion was half propping him up, but there was so much blood on both men that only the pallor showed which was hurt. I phoned for the duty doctor, and my colleague took the dripping pair into casualty, leaving a trail of blood all the way. Waiting for the GP, who was aware of how urgent it was, we tried to find where all the blood was coming from. The injured man had bet the other that he could smash the glass in telephone kiosks without being hurt. The first two were all right but the third was his undoing, and this had sobered up his mate enough to know that help was needed, fast. But a drunken, bleeding man isn't very fast-moving, so the more sober one tied his lanyard as a tourniquet round the gashed forearm. The trouble was he'd no idea how long ago he'd tied it. We'd been taught to release a tourniquet very slowly when the length of time was doubtful, so we tried to do it. Hot, sticky, human blood coming from a man whose breath could have been ignited with a match, combined with the sour smell of frightened sweat on a hot night, made us feel nauseated. The man wouldn't keep still long enough for us to try to find the knot, let alone untie it, so we cut the lanyard and were heartily abused by the owner as we did so. The blood pumped out with the release of pressure, so it was a great relief to hear the GP's footsteps hurrying to us. It took almost all our combined strengths to hold on to the man for the doctor to locate the worst bleeding point and tie it off. The rest would clot eventually and were fairly superficial. We had more or less to sit on both men, so plenty of blood was transferred to us. Even with three sober and one semi-sober, it was impossible to do a proper job. As fast as the skin stitches were put in the cut, the man pulled them out with the other hand and threw them up into the air with drunken shrieks. His strength was enormous, but he couldn't be given any drugs on top of his alcohol intake so we put on layers of dressings and covered the rest with elastoplast that would take a lot of shifting. There was no way we could keep him for the night, so he was despatched to the police cells for the police surgeon to assess and transfer him to a bigger hospital if he needed a transfusion, otherwise he was to come back for proper stitching next morning.

Clearing up all the mess took ages, everywhere had been liberally bespattered with blood, inside and out. Next day a trail was found from the kiosk to the hospital front door; we didn't volunteer to clean that up! We were told that a very subdued man came back, but still furious about his mate's cut lanyard which he would have to replace. Hard luck! I never found out what the GPO or Fleet Air Arm did about it.

Another man was found groaning in the gutter one night, so we had to admit him. He'd hit his head in falling or had been kicked. Residents nearby had heard a noisy fight and running feet. This man was fighting drunk, and impossible to undress as he was too obstreperous and strong. He spent the night shouting, 'Get off, you b–,' in between vomiting, first on one side of the bed and then the other. We were sickened by it all and so were the rest of the patients. In the morning he insisted on getting up, although most unfit to do so, but he was going home and no-one could stop him. Luckily the day staff came and took over. He utterly refused to have his head X-rayed or any other investigations. Within a month he dropped dead, there had been a skull fracture there all the time, but he'd let no-one help him. Enquiries had to be started to find out the real facts of the night, but we heard no more.

Firework night brought the inevitable spate of injuries, caused largely by careless behaviour. Mishandling and deliberate throwing of lighted fireworks always seemed to hurt the innocent.

One lad had been passing a group of older boys when one of them threw a lighted banger straight at him. He was unable to duck in time and it had hit his face, with one eye getting the full force. It was an awful mess, with burnt furrows and craters in it. All we could do was wash it out with saline, cover it and send him to a specialist unit by ambulance. He begged us not to tell his mother as she'd had, or was about to have, a new baby, so we phoned his father, leaving him to tell his wife. If we could have got hold of the thrower he would have thought twice about doing it again.

A bit of light relief, which could have been serious, but wasn't, came along later. A plump woman with a teenaged daughter came in gasping what sounded like, 'Me bum's alight, I tell you, alight.' Sure enough that is what she was saying, and when we got under her several layers we found charred patches on her underwear and a scorch mark on one buttock. They'd been walking along when a firecracker jumped up under her skirt. She shrieked, first with fright and then with pain, clapped her hands to her bottom and told all and sundry that her bum was alight. Her daughter didn't appreciate what was happening, but a passer-by, a Scot, said, 'Sit doon, ma guid wumman, it'll put the wee fire oot,' and gave her a downward thrust (he came to tell us this later) and his push along with the thickness of her clothes, saved her from a bad burn. No-one blamed her for being frightened though.

The months went by and I tried to stifle the urge which told me to go ahead and do the SRN course at the local hospital. Finally the matron, who had guessed at my inner confusion without my realising, told me not to be a fool but to go ahead and stop hesitating. So I was interviewed and accepted for two and a half years' training, getting six months off for my SEN qualification, providing I took and passed the State Prelim within the first six months, otherwise I would have to do the full three years. So once again the die was cast.

6

Papers and Prizes

I supposed that I would settle eventually and put study behind me before I reached old age as I started three months in the Preliminary Training School. All the others were young enough to be my daughters, if I'd married early, but we got on well together, and surprisingly the study was far less hard than I'd imagined it would be, and all my experience was of great value. Those three months sped by, with Christmas in the middle. No hair-raising cycle rides in the dark for me, we all had some leave at home.

Towards the end of the time we had to take and pass an exam before being sent on to a ward. Failure meant either opting for the SEN course, or leaving to start a life away from nursing, for all expect me, as I was already an SEN. With this behind me I was sent to male medical ward, and before I knew it, back on night duty! In theory I was the middle nurse, relieving both senior and junior on their nights off. The junior had been in place longer than I, but as I had a qualification I was her senior. This counted with the powers that be when convenient, but was just as conveniently forgotten. I seemed to be left without a junior most nights, leaving me with a male orderly, the only man I've ever met who could fall asleep at any time, in any place, as when buttering bread, or over the bedpan washer when emptying used receptacles.

The night super told me it was my job to keep the orderly awake, and I should try to find a subject which interested him. Luckily, or so I rashly thought, I knew he loved cricket, going to matches when he should have been sleeping ready for a night's work ahead. So, one night I sat opposite him in the middle of the ward to do as commanded. The MCC had a winter tour to somewhere, so trying not to disturb the patients, I started to talk about our team's performance. It was useless, as he kept dropping off, so I had to raise my voice to penetrate his sleepy mind. It wasn't him I awakened but a patient near by, who said the thing about women was that they would talk about games they knew nothing of. That stung, because cricket was a game I did know about. Having failed so dismally to get the orderly awake, I resorted to giving him a smartish tap on the head when I heard the night sister's footsteps. He jumped to his feet, rushed to the sluice, came back with a urinal and went to a patient at random, finding him fast asleep. Just as Sister came into the ward he came to me with a face like thunder and said, 'The silly b– didn't want it.' By that time I couldn't even raise an inward laugh. I was getting rather sick of him and knew that they would never have put a younger nurse on duty with him, as he never pulled his weight. However, in some ways I preferred his all-night snoring while I worked to being on duty with the senior, who gave, unasked, details of her lurid sex life which, if true, would have been unfit to publish in the most sordid magazine.

In the side ward was a Nonconformist minister recovering from a heart attack. Going in with his breakfast tray, I failed to notice the bed wheels were turned to stick out in the room. In such a confined space there was no room for my feet and the wheels, so I tripped, depositing the tray on his chest. I was so afraid I'd given him another attack through shock, but he assured me he was better, even if no-one else believed him. He was a very nice man and told no-one else what I'd done. One Sunday, ages afterwards, we had what is known in the Free Church as an exchange of pulpits, so that instead of the usual man, we had one from another local church. There in the pulpit was my ex-patient. My sister and I nearly had to leave in a fit of laughter when I whispered, 'I bet I'm the only one here who has shot a breakfast tray over him and blanket-bathed him.' After the service he was at the door, shaking hands. Recognition dawned and with a twinkle in his eye said, 'We meet under different circumstances today, eh?'

I enjoyed life on woman's surgical ward from the word go, and go it was, all the time. We all worked harder than I thought possible and yet remained upright at the end of duty, but it was very satisfying.

Regrets came when people died, in spite of all that was done to prevent this, but nursing them was a challenge of skill, knowledge, patience and one's own temperament. It made me realise in a new way that a nurse, to help the whole person, must be a good listener. Mental anguish and worry about home and the family were often harder for them to bear than the physical pain. A sixth sense used to come to some who knew they weren't going to pull through and all sorts of questions were asked. Some I couldn't answer, others I could, but was in no position to do so, and I felt totally helpless. In some ways I was at a disadvantage, age-wise on a par with the senior staff, many of whom had been trained when listening and talking were not considered part of a nurse's work, doing was all that mattered, yet my training was in and with a very different age. I felt with my young contemporaries that people mattered more than petty details. Of course discipline counted, so did having orderly equipment in the right place as a life might depend on this. These were not the things we resented, it was the petty niggling rules, accepted for far too long without question.

Being a non-smoker, I must confess to being thoroughly intolerant of the selfishness of smokers, never more so than on a surgical ward. Both men and women had their surreptitious drags in the lavatories, some right up to the time of their pre-operative sedation. Afterwards, when trying to rid their lungs of the anaesthetic, they had to have far more time spent on them by the physiotherapists, and us, than the non-smokers. We kept up inhalations in between breathing exercises, but even then pneumonia could develop, meaning a longer stay and more misery than they'd bargained for. Then just as they were less breathless, beginning to taste food again and their breath was less offensive to smell, they'd nearly always start smoking again. To me it seemed such waste of time and energy and money to get them well enough to start the cycle all over again.

Lectures had to be attended all through our training, but not in off-duty, so ward rosters had to be made to include both. Some of the sisters felt glad that it was different from their day when off-duty didn't matter, but others said we would never be the nurses they were as our training was too soft! It made no difference what anyone thought, we all had to have our off-duty and lecture time.

My six months were almost finished, so I had to leave the group I'd started with as their exam would not be for another six months, and join the group which had started before us. I didn't particularly like leaving my set, but soon got on with the others and took the State Prelim, practical and written. When the results came through and we knew we'd passed, we had to go to the matron for a pep talk on what sort of nurses we should hope to be in our second year, and to be given a belt to show our new rank.

I did my time in theatre between night and day duties, very grateful for the bit of experience I'd had. The pace was alarming, and without the past I would have been daunted. We all had to take turns to be on call, with a regular night sister, for any emergency. This meant sleeping in the hospital for the night. My one prayer was, 'Please don't let there be an emergency tonight.' This was always answered until I was on nights on Women's Surgical. The night sister would always call me from the ward duties to help her; she said I'd got common sense and didn't flap. If only she'd known how I really felt! It would have been a great experience for anyone who loved theatre work. I tried to concentrate on the operation while my thoughts were with the junior nurse I'd left behind on the ward, and wondered how she was coping. Some surgical registrars seemed to love having patients admitted at night, extra beds often being put down in the middle of wards. Essential, but inconvenient to other patients and staff alike. The only happy person was the one practising his or her surgery.

Night duty was a very good way to lose weight, as we all did it with jaded appetites and untempting food. Even though we came off duty at 8 a.m., after 12 hours on duty, it was still morning, but we got given the night before's supper menu. To be confronted at that time with shepherd's pie, boiled cabbage, fried onions, stew, boiled puddings and the like was impossible. I at least had a choice as I lived at home, for there I'd have a proper breakfast. I used to cycle home in the fresh air, which went to my head after the night on the ward with all the accompanying smells, knowing that Mother would have an appetising breakfast for me. Then a hot bath, and the utter bliss of stretching out in my own bed. I'd not have changed places with anyone.

If a really serious accident came in at night, the theatre sister had to call as many nurses from the wards as needed; this was rare but road traffic accidents could involve many of us.

One evening there was a gale blowing and booming as I cycled off from home. It was hard to keep upright and the sea was hissing and roaring on the shingle. Such a night meant trees blown down, small boats seeking shelter and moored ones breaking loose. At the hospital everything that could rattle did, continuously. The wind seemed to threaten the south-facing windows, so we did the last routine at a leisurely pace, knowing that the patients would take a long time to settle. We had just about finished when the phone rang. I was told to see that the junior knew what to do and which night sister to contact, and then get down to Casualty, where a major accident was on the way. I hurried off to join the rest who had been called. The wail of the ambulance sirens could be heard getting nearer, and soon three stretchers were brought in. It looked like a mine disaster: all three were black, and there was a strong smell of soot around.

They were a mother and her two young sons on holiday from New Zealand to see relatives here. They'd rented a holiday flat at the top of a five-storey Regency house, right opposite the sea. An extra-strong gust of wind had brought the chimneystack right through the roof, with the masonry falling on top of the boys' bed. With this came an avalanche of ancient soot, which had liberally covered both boys and their mother as she rushed in to see what was happening.

She wasn't hurt, but very shocked and anxious. Until we got some of the soot off it was impossible to tell how badly hurt, or not, the boys were. No-one who has never tried to wash off soot can know how difficult it is, it merely floats off and stays on top of the water. The shallow breathing and pulse of one boy soon showed which was hurt; the other was deeply shocked, but with no apparent injury. A surgeon and anaesthetist had been sent for as soon as the alert had been received, and the theatre was ready, so all we had to do was to get the boy out of his sooty pyjamas, wash his face and mouth free from the all-pervading black powder, and get him to theatre as soon as possible. He begged for a drink and to spend a penny. Both had to be denied him till after surgery, for the doctor on call thought the injury was low down, possibly involving the bladder, though there was no external sign.

It was a long, delicate operation, for the masonry had crushed his urethra. The damaged piece had to be removed, the two ends rejoined and a catheter inserted so that no urine would flow over the join and stop the healing. It was several weeks before he was well, but eventually they all went home. Meanwhile we were left with the other boy, the mother, and that soot and all the mess to clear up. Once the mother knew that her injured son was in good hands and the other unhurt, she gallantly helped us all she could. The smell of soot would not go, and no matter how we tried, we couldn't get rid of the dirty, greasy tidemarks on all the equipment we'd used. For the rest of the night we reeked of soot too. I'm sure the day staff thought our cleaning rather inadequate, but we all had to get back to our wards. It said a lot for the younger ones we'd left to hold the fort that they had coped with everything and not moaned about the time we'd been away.

I did four months' night duty on that challenging ward, and quite regretted having to change to get on with my training.

In my two and a half years I had experience in all the departments and wards, even almost enjoying a second dose of theatre, though I knew it was no place for me to work in when training was finished. There was a team spirit there in a different way from ward work, rank wasn't so keenly felt, everyone just had to get on with all routine as well as the intricacies of surgery. Outpatients and Casualty were places to endure working in, but not for long term.

On Ear, Nose and Throat (ENT) I had my second experience with a man who had a tracheotomy, i.e. a tube inserted into the windpipe. Such an operation, with the drama of kitchen tables and diphtheria, used to be beloved by romantic fiction writers. It was indeed a lifesaver then, but is now used far more frequently in all conditions where breathing is impaired either temporarily or permanently. Many polio victims could have been saved – many were – by this simple operation. A great many road traffic victims too have been saved by this one measure.

My first patient had been in the little

country hospital, a big man with a huge cancerous growth in his neck, with secondary deposits distorting his neck and face more and more. Never having seen anything like this, except leprosy in India, I was more afraid than repulsed. He was so cheerful, in spite of intense discomfort and pain, and very patient with my first blundering efforts to remove his tube, wash and replace it. He put his thumb over the hole in his throat to give a weak, husky, but understandable voice when the tube was out, and gave me encouragement along with precise instructions, until my fears left me. He taught me all I needed to know about tracheotomies, and his courage, patience and smile taught me never-to-be-forgotten lessons, so I counted it as a privilege, albeit a sad one, to be with him when he died.

So, armed with this inner confidence, I stood silently by the ward sister as she showed me what to do for the man who had cancer of the throat. By then I'd learned to keep quiet about anything I'd done as an

SEN. There were still so many who would not recognise that status, that is until times of staff shortages and stress, when it was expedient to remember that we had reached a certain standard of training. The poor man had so much of his jaw and neck eroded by the disease, which was still eating away the flesh, that there was a hole through which could be seen large, fragile, pulsating blood vessels, and the stench was dreadful. He had to be made comfortable and though I'd been warned that he wouldn't allow some nurses, particularly new ones, to touch him, I hoped that my first efforts would not upset him. Things went smoothly and well, thanks to my old friend's lesson, and after that I always did his dressings when I was on duty. Once again, I had to hand it to the young ones, who, with very few exceptions, were very cheerful and kind to the most nauseatingly ill patients. I doubted whether I could have been so tolerant at 19 or 20 years of age. We admired the relatives of such ill people; how they managed to control their emotions and talk cheerfully and hopefully when they knew there was no hope, I'll never know.

A post-operative unit had been set up in a stately mansion on the other side of town and all students had to spend some time there. The house, with its grounds, was beautiful, the hall paved with alternative black and white marble squares. One ward was bedecked with gold leaf and lovely plasterwork, it seemed a crime to fasten cubicle curtain rails to the walls. There was a lake with an island where ducks nested, plus a bad-tempered swan. It was a delightful place to recover from surgery in, but not so delectable for the nurses and staff who worked upstairs in the women's wards. Oh, the stairs we had to climb! There were several different levels once we'd got up there and we spent our time going up and down them. The food came up from the kitchen below, in a lift pulled up by a rope, so trays had to be taken to each patient, set with cutlery, before their food arrived. The furthest ward was 16 stairs away from the serving place, and of course, 16 back. With large, heavy trays, heavier still with plates of food covered in aluminium covers, it was no easy task to keep it all on the trays, and very tiring. One day, when Sister was serving the main meal, one of us said how hard the stairs seemed at meal times. Quick as a flash she said, 'Be like me, run up them two at a time, then you won't feel them so much.' This was so unfair that my reply came just as quickly. 'It's easy for you, Sister, you never carry anything heavier than a book with all the patients' names in. You try running up and down, two at a time, with laden trays.' The serving spoon stayed poised over the dish in dead silence, while I was given a long, searching look and we all wondered what was coming. We breathed again when she conceded that I had a point, and we heard no more of 'two at a time'.

This house was suitable for those who were going to recover and getting more mobile daily, but it gradually became a place where the main hospital sent patients who could not recover. Far from getting mobile, they became very heavy nursing cases: incontinent, completely helpless, and not at all suitable for nursing in such an inconvenient place. None of the equipment was geared for such nursing. The casualty officer slept there and did a round every day before he set off for the hospital, but medical help during the day was no closer than a phone call and a quick dash, through traffic, across town. The one small lift didn't go right to the top of the house, and it was a pinch to get one small wheelchair and another person standing in it.

It was a ghastly thing when anyone upstairs died at night. No porter was available at night, the two on days were neither young nor fit either. We had to carry a body down in a canvas sling, the one in front holding the body high, while the one behind was nearly bent double. It was very hard to stop a heavy body from slipping out. Where, oh where, was the dignity in death about which we were constantly lectured? The mortuary was outside, at the end of an ornamental terrace, in full view of all passers-by in daytime, and very inconvenient at night, as the rest had to be left without a nurse until we'd transferred the body.

However, food at this place was marvellous, making a great difference to the spirits as well as health of all concerned, so we hated going back to the food of the main hospital.

My third year came incredibly quickly and in no time I'd taken the hospital final exams and the State Final was in the offing. The results of the hospital exams came while I was working in theatre again. I got top marks for several papers, ensuring me of more prizes to go with those I'd been awarded on the two previous prize-givings. The surgeon who lectured us in ENT and marked the papers had a gruff but kindly voice which was hard to catch when he was masked and operating. We had got through the operating list one morning when he turned to the theatre superintendent and said, 'Had an excellent paper from one of the students, never had one like it before. I didn't know how to mark it and not give full marks, but thought I'd better take off one or two. Any idea who it might be, Sister?' I was about to slink into the sluice but Sister said, 'No, but this nurse will, she took the exam.' 'Oh who then?' he asked. 'Please sir, it was me,' I said, meekly for me. His eyes twinkled over the top of his mask and he said, 'I'm sure I never taught you all that. Where did you get it from?' 'From having lived longer than the others and by being observant,' was all I could think of to say.

The paediatrician was equally complimentary about his paper so I felt glad that I'd more than held my own among the younger brains. At last I'd done something really positive with my life. Four prizes were coming to me on the next Prize Day and to crown it all I was awarded the Gold Medal as best nurse of the year. Whoever would have thought of such a thing when I started nursing just as a means of earning my living.

The State Final results came when I was on night duty, the post arrived early in the morning and we'd been told to report at a given time to the sister tutor in the front hall on the fateful day. Suddenly I felt apprehensive. What if I'd failed after all? Rather diffidently I went as ordered, leaving the junior on the ward. Seeing the sister tutor's face round the corner, I stopped, but she said, 'Come along, Nurse. What are you hanging back for, you know you've passed.' How can you be so sure, I thought, as I opened my envelope. But she was right. I had passed.

7

SRN

Matron decided to which ward or department the newly qualified SRNs would go. I was put on Women's Surgical as third staff nurse. The other two were fine as individuals, but together impossible as they had a running feud and I wondered how long I'd be able to stand being piggy in the middle.

Apart from the main buildings was an old school, the top floor of which was used as a women's geriatric ward. The sister in charge had a car crash which would keep her away for several weeks, so I was sent to take charge until she returned. I knew it was only a temporary thing but it suited me to be able to do things without first asking, and to have relief from being the butt between the other two. There was one nurse, like me older than the rest, who would persist in talking baby talk to the old ladies. 'Have a bit of toasty woasty with the eggy peggy,' was her breakfast favourite, but it only seemed to irk me, not them. Perhaps they'd grown too apathetic to care, but it so grated on me that I could only think of her as 'Nursey Wursey', almost forgetting her real name.

It was a constant battle to keep these old ladies in dry beds. Those with indwelling catheters were easy, but for the rest it was a constant bedpan round. One Sunday morning there was a TV service to celebrate the long years of the Church Missionary Society, the distinguished visitors included the Queen Mother and Archbishop of Canterbury among many other church and state dignitaries. One old lady refused a bedpan before the service started so her bed was awash afterwards and had to be changed before lunch could be served. To my query, 'Why didn't you ask for one? No-one would have been angry even though you'd refused one earlier,' she replied, with outraged dignity, 'What, in front of the Queen Mother, all those men, and in church – I'm surprised at you!' Even I could think of no answer to that.

When the time came for me to relinquish my temporary post and go back to my ward, I found to my delight that one of the other staff nurses had gone back to her native Scotland and the other had asked to work on a male ward. My promotion to senior staff nurse had been swift, but I had no objections. I was happy with the responsibility, even though the work was very taxing.

The stamina and courage of patients continued to amaze me, their uncomplaining endurance, sometimes at very advanced ages, after severe surgery, was very humbling. At one time we had an old lady of Romany extraction. The fact that it was well diluted with non-Romany marriages in no way diminished her pride. She always felt she had the edge over all the rest and any newcomers. We were all put in our place by her, but nobody minded, as she was so unconsciously funny. Alternate weekends were worked by the sister and me. Being on duty from midday Friday to 4.30 p.m. Monday was a long stint. One Saturday afternoon an emergency was admitted, so the Romany started telling her what was what. The trouble was, the new patient was deaf and her hearing aid had been left at home in the rush, so she alone heard nothing of the remarks being shouted across the ward. The doctor on call, with me as chaperone, went behind the curtains to start what became a long, negative session. In the end it seemed that surgery was not essential at once, so the daughter went home for the hearing aid and all the other things left behind.

Monday morning, with Sister back on duty, we walked down the ward, with me giving a verbal report on each patient. The old Romany beckoned with an imperious finger, saying, 'Sister, the thing what goes on when you ain't 'ere is nobody's business. What was they doing behind them curtains all that time? I ain't never seen that man in a white coat before. 'e 'ad one of them tubes in 'is pocket, so I spose 'e was some kind of doctor, but they was behind them curtains for a long time, and I knows that doctors is men and nurses is women!' The fact that the man in question was years younger than I, and all we'd said to the deaf patient could have been heard a mile away, meant nothing to her, and what about the other 23 patients?

Among the house surgeons was a Scot, who on high days and holidays wore the kilt with pride. He was a great rugger player, his legs hairy and muscular, who enjoyed his drink and was merrily unpredictable but never offensive. A patient, still hazy from her anaesthetic which was wearing off, saw the hairy legs beneath the kilt and said in a remote voice, 'Why doesn't that doctor wear a longer skirt? I've never seen a lady with such legs!' The Scot joined in with the laughter and tried to explain his sex and garb, but the patient was still too doped to take it in and before dropping off again said, 'And why is she wearing woolly socks? It's not a cold day!' The next day she didn't recognise him in conventional male dress.

On Christmas Eve we toured the wards with our cloaks inside out to show the red linings, singing carols, with lighted candles in jam jars. As we left the main building to go across to the maternity block, there was a cry from the Scot, 'Ma light's gone oot, ma light's gone oot.' Someone relit his candle and evoked childhood memories, for he started singing, 'Jesus bids us shine with a clear, pure light, like a little candle burning in the night.' He couldn't remember any more, and just as well, for the rest of us were well into the next carol, his strident voice ringing out above us all. Matron, at the front of the procession, looked back disapprovingly at the tail, where we were trying unsuccessfully to keep the merriment down. The climax came when we trooped over to the geriatric block. In a lull in the singing, while we were looking for the next carol on the sheet, came the same Scot's plaintive voice, 'There's an awfu' smell o' wee-wee here!' That nearly brought the house down, it was so true. But it was obvious that a different form of Christmas spirit was taking over some of the carollers, so we disbanded.

Prize-giving came in July, and I, as Gold Medallist, had to make a speech. Rarely at a loss for words, I had to decide what to say publicly, briefly and politely to all concerned in our training. Their standards had varied so, and some we had no cause to feel many thanks for. Still, I managed it, sounding a complete stranger when I heard the reply. Mother lived long enough to know this climax of my training, but died very unexpectedly soon after.

I don't think I had my full wits about me when I applied for, and got, a post as relief sister. Semi-perpetual night duty was my lot, with never any part of any weekend free.

As a student on nights I'd slept through sheer physical exhaustion, but life was so different now. I was awakened by every sound, resenting dogs' barks when our own were silent. For me life had lost its sparkle with this promotion. I was no longer doing the work I enjoyed as I was on the outside of practical nursing, and that was not for me. My sister and I had almost got to the stage of saying hello and goodbye as we met on the stairs, one going as the other arrived. Coming home to an empty house after the night made my mother's absence strike me more and more as the weeks went by. I knew I must alter this situation before it altered me as a person; I neither liked myself nor my work.

Seemingly out of the blue I heard that there would shortly be a vacancy, through retirement, on the local District Nursing Service. Was this what I wanted? During our training we had all spent part of a day with one of the district nurses and I'd loved it. I wrote to the senior nursing officer (all titles changed with the NHS reorganisation later), had an interview with her and the MOH, and was accepted for the post in three months' time.

The thought of spending three more months doing a job I'd come to loathe was more than I could contemplate, so I resigned. This meant three months without pay, but the dissatisfaction I felt could not be ignored. Once I'd decided to leave I felt on top of the world, ready to face the new job when the time came. My colleagues were aghast at my improvidence, my pension would be ruined etc. Nothing they said could make any difference, I was once again going to nurse, not be a filler-in of endless forms and lists or a continual answerer of phones. All these had to be done, but not by me. The only part I knew I'd miss was passing on the skills and knowledge I'd acquired to the students. If I'd started earlier, or more truthfully, stuck it out from my first starting, I should have liked to have been a sister tutor. On the other hand, my life had shaped me into what I now was, so who knows? Strangely, after all they said, several of my hospital colleagues joined me on the District later.

So I started on the last phase of my nursing life, the part that gave me more happiness and fulfilment than I'd thought possible. What more could anyone ask?

8

On the District

What was once the District is now the Community Nursing Service, and all staff have to undergo a course of special training for it. When I joined, this was not the case; newcomers were taken round with an experienced nurse, the length of time depending on how quickly the essentials were grasped. There was always someone else to ask, so it wasn't long before I was out on my own. Three of us worked part of the time, each relieving the others' off duty. The whole town was divided thus.

In time we all got to know all the patients in our area. I started on a bike, in due course learning to drive and having the luxury of a county car. During the first weeks, just as I'd begun to get the hang of things, relieving the other two seemed to throw me back. I got used to my own patients but the others, seen only once a week, were a different matter. The only non-changing duty was that all diabetic patients were visited first, as their insulin was the priority. Every day at first seemed to bring some problem or situation that made me unsure, but my senior had a faith in me which I hoped was not going to be misplaced. Some people thought that I should be at a disadvantage nursing in my home town where my family had been for generations, and where I was known by many. But I never found it to be anything but a bonus, I never lost my way, could take all the short cuts known from childhood, and met many people who knew my family. Family news made mutual talking points, making me wish I'd got one parent alive, they'd have been so interested. I had to be content with telling my elderly, very alert aunt any bits of interest. I revelled in the fact that I was doing real nursing again. It was so different from in hospital, where patients were captives, as it were. Relations and friends were only seen at visiting times, but in patients' homes, we were the visitors. Here we couldn't dictate, only wheedle, coerce or plead to get our own way, for the patient's benefit, not ours.

Gradually I found my feet, able, as I gained experience, to assess situations more confidently. I learned to adapt, as had all the others, to many things I'd not thought about in hospital nursing. Feather beds, double beds, masses of furniture to walk round, an ordinary amount of household linen instead of the extravagance of hospital supplies, made me realise how out of touch with reality that sort of nursing was. In the home, if one partner of a marriage had always slept on one side of the bed, illness made no difference, he/she might be incontinent and dying, but we had to accept that the other one would continue to share the bed, however inconvenient and distressing it might be. Sometimes it was hard to keep both dry, but the well ones never seemed to resent things. Most of our patients were in the elderly bracket and had grown tolerant of each other in their years together. For the most part the beds were old-fashioned and high, a good height for nursing and easier to get out of than in, but we didn't have to heave and wrench from low divans where only toes would go under. A dining chair placed at a strategic angle made a good backrest, and an oval pie dish a satisfactory female urinal in an emergency.

Soon I felt as though I'd been in the job for years. But this feeling received a severe jolt one morning. I was cycling along when a man rushed up, nearly knocking me over. 'Come quickly, Nurse. My wife has cut her throat,' he gasped. My heart thumped with trepidation, this was more than I'd bargained for! So, trying to look calm and unconcerned, as though I was used to such drama, I put my bike against the wall, grabbed my bag and followed the man. In the back room was a white-faced, muttering, distraught woman with an ominous red line round her neck. But it was only oozing, not gushing, so was obviously not deep. All the same, it was alarming to her husband and me, so I said, 'I'll go to the phone box and get your doctor to come.' 'No, Nurse, I'll phone, you stay,' he said, and went, leaving me with no saliva or a practical thought in my head.

Someone once said that when a nurse doesn't know what to do, she starts to wash the patient. That day I found there was truth in that. One can talk normally doing an ordinary thing like washing a face and hands, without further upset to a disturbed person. I got some water and started to wash the dried blood off. Talking without saliva was a bit hard, but when the poor soul relaxed and wept shuddering tears, my fears left me. I could have joined in her distress and wept too! I stayed until the doctor came and the ambulance took her to the mental hospital, where she remained until her death. Then I had to sit and let the man unburden himself over a welcome cup of tea.

I felt like going home to get over the shock but had too many others waiting for me, and I was very late. I had no time to dwell on the episode, so I got it in perspective, hoping that it was a non-repetitive strand of life.

I had never really thought about toenails until I went into people's homes. Some had been left to grow so long that they had become tubes, all turned round like rams' horns. One woman, whose shoe size should have been a size five, had had to resort to a man's size eight to accommodate her nails. I had been sent to her after her husband had told the GP that this wife had been in bed for a week, and wouldn't get up to do the cooking etc. She had had a stroke and was partly paralysed and incontinent. The husband was elderly, very confused and unable to cope with anything. Neither could I without help, for the state of her bed and person was yet another eye-opener to me! I just didn't know how to begin, so I arranged with a colleague to join me, and in the meantime managed to get some water hot and find a selection of ancient sheets, towels and night things. Four changes of water started to show the real colour of her skin, but as we washed her filthy feet, the long nails broke right off, with no hint of pain. The colour of his wife's hair amazed the old man, he'd got so used to seeing the dirty, unwashed head, that the superfine white hair was as much of a revelation to him as to us.

To save him the continual journeys up and down stairs, we asked his permission to bring a single bed down to the front room. When he said yes we realised the amount of furniture already there: a piano, china cabinet, small chairs, stuffed 'easy' ones and a table. By dint of moving out what we could, and by pushing what we couldn't against the walls, we made room for the bed to be squeezed against the one free wall. It was a very awkward arrangement and a twice-daily battle with constricted space and furniture.

Calling out, as I always did when I went in, a muffled reply came from the front room, sounding so odd that I didn't wait to take my coat off. The bed was at a funny angle, the patient out of sight. From below came, 'My 'ead don't arf feel queer down 'ere, the bed's gorn through the floor.' So there she was, the top half lower than the bottom. The floorboards had been unable to take the weight of the bed and patient and our twice-daily tramping around. I couldn't lift her or the bed on my own, so I flew out into the road to find a strong arm. This was given me by a wiling postman, so intrigued that he simply had to see. We did a sort of war dance to find sounder flooring, no easy task with so much furniture; the poor husband kept saying, 'Oh, my, what a carry-on!' The only sound bit of flooring left us with a climb over the bed every time we wanted the other side, almost landing on the unmoveable piano. It was a very good day for everyone when she was admitted to hospital, for with the best will in the world we could never have got her walking again, there just was no room.

Evening calls in the winter soon taught me to carry a torch. One dark evening I had been sent to a house still lit by gas. I'd thought this a thing of the past, but found that there were still a number of houses without electricity. Only when town gas was replaced with natural gas was the situation altered. Not even the obstinacy of tenants or landlords could stand out against that.

The house I went into was in complete darkness. Torchlight showed me no light switch in the hall, my repeated calls brought no answer, and it was most eerie. In the large front room I saw gaslights, with shades, on either side of the mantelpiece, and a double bed, unoccupied, against one wall. Still calling, 'Is anyone there?' I went into the next room. Like the front, it had a bed with no-one in it! The first two bedrooms upstairs had the now familiar empty double beds. I wondered who had slept in them all. Four rooms done, just one more to go. By then I was feeling uneasy and began to prepare myself for a body, or something unpleasant, in the last room. Torchlight showed yet another bed, but no body. Feeling utterly mystified I turned to go when my ankle was clutched by a cold, bony hand from under the bed. I was nearly sick with fright but knelt down to look. There was the woman I'd come to see, looking clean and well nourished. The bedding was good and plentiful and she seemed very comfortable. 'You come under here with me, you'll be safe from the bombs,' she said, still clutching my ankle. For her the war wasn't 20 years ago, it was still present. She wouldn't come out and I wouldn't go under, so with a struggle I got my ankle out of her grasp and went to see the GP, who I found had never seen her. She was on his list, as was her neighbour, who had told him that the old lady was 'acting peculiar'. It was on this basis alone he'd sent me. She certainly didn't need any help, her shopping was done for her, she wasn't short of money, and if she chose to sleep under the bed (with five to choose from!) she was doing no harm.

Having a car made a great difference, especially in wet weather, but just before I finished cycling I had to go to one of my male colleague's patients whose wife needed support. It was a drenching day, and I was soaked and dripping wet as I rang the front doorbell. I was firmly sent round to the back door, as though I was a Sairey Gamp, not a trained nurse. I got no further than the kitchen door. 'You can't come in, you are dripping on my carpet, and if you hang up your coat, it will still drip. Why are you wet?' I pointed out, in a milder way than I felt, that it was raining hard and, on a bike, I couldn't keep dry. All she reiterated was that I was wet, dripping on her carpets, and that my feet were wet – as if I needed any telling – and that she was not prepared to put up with it. I gave her the choice of having me wet or not at all. She chose the latter, so I went to her GP and told him. I felt rather anxious; after all, for the first time I'd been refused to see a patient. His reaction comforted me; he was more concerned about my wet state than that the man had not had a visit. I was glad I'd not got that reception in every home.

My first car was a Mini, very easy to park in the town centre. One morning I was visiting a patient who lived in a cul-de-sac. No other cars were in the road when I parked and went in, but when I came out, one was parked hard up against my front and another at the back. There was no way I could move. A dustcart had been in the road from the start – the men had spoken to me as I parked. They saw my dilemma as I tried to drive away, and their language about the two other drivers was very much to the point! Telling me to get out, the six hefty men picked up my Mini, moved it so that they could turn it round and said, 'There you are, ducks.' Their kindness was beyond thanks, but I met with a lot of kindness, including from traffic wardens. Everyone knew how hard it was to park in the town centre, and that's where many patients lived.

One large woman in the area the three of us covered, but whom I only saw on the others' days off, had put herself to bed with a 'bad leg' years before. She stayed there, ruling the household of niece and nephew in a despotic way. Nothing that went on in the road was missed by her, she saw it all from behind lace curtains. Her room was the front one downstairs, with kitchen and scullery behind. One Saturday morning I was greeted with a strong waft of onions when I went into the scullery for the hot water, there stood jars and peeled onions, waiting for the spiced vinegar. The niece always washed her aunt's face and hands. The rest was left for us, and the leg to dress. I'd got everything, including a clean drawsheet, ready when I was told, 'When you washes my bum, pick out the pickling spices. I dropped it all last night, it'll be all right when it's washed.' Her enormous buttocks were embedded with peppercorns, chillies, bits of ginger and cloves. It had all been under her all night, so she was pitted by the hard spices. She gave me a plate to put the loot on, but I only put a token amount of it, shooting the bulk into the water that she couldn't see. When she saw my meagre collection she was surprised at the smallness, but grabbed it and called for her long-suffering niece to fetch it, wash it and 'shove it in the vinegar'. I shot the bowl's contents down the sink quickly and rinsed it very well in case a lurking peppercorn gave the game away. My next visit to her produced a jar of picked onions for me. It was put in the first rubbish bin I found.

A very observant woman was this one, not only about her neighbours, but us too. 'My nurse wore 'er 'at,' she told me one day. This didn't seem very earth-shattering news, we were all supposed to wear hats on duty. 'Noticed 'er 'air was getting grey at the roots agen.' Next time I visited I was informed, 'she never 'ad 'er 'at at all this week, she'd 'ad it done.' I wonder what little bits of gossip she passed on to the others about me, but I always wore my hat and didn't dye my hair!

The time eventually came when the bed-springs broke under her weight, so a generous second-hand dealer gave her a bed with good castors. We could move the bed away from the wall, so it was much easier for us to manage than before. Ambulance men had to come to lift her from one bed to the next, and to the good lady's pleasure the new bed was quite a bit higher than the old, so her view from behind the Victorian lace was wider, and our backs didn't suffer.

9

Pet Owners and Other Eccentrics

Animals and birds played a great part in many patients' lives; often they kept the lonely from becoming withdrawn and senile. One patient, neither withdrawn or senile, lived in a large town house, and an Alsatian was part of the household. One day I thought I heard a lamb's bleat but it seemed so incongruous in a town house, with a large dog, that I thought it was my imagination. But a loud bleat was unmistakeable and down the stairs bowled a fat lamb, followed by the Alsatian. It was an orphan from a friend's farm with no-one able to feed it regularly. So there it lived, getting ever fatter and more stubborn as the weeks passed. It refused to settle in the farm when large enough to fend for itself, and in the end had to be put down because of intractable bowel parasites. This sort of unexpectedness helped to make the work amusing.

At another house we were always greeted by a large black and white rabbit lolloping along the passage, his feet slithering on the shiny lino. He was far from house trained, but this didn't bother the old lady as her house was so squalid that rabbit droppings only adding marginally to the mess. In another town house a big buck rabbit lived in perfect harmony with the family's Alsatian, they both lay together on their own settee. Each time the dog went into the garden the rabbit went too, and there was never any mess night or day. The only drawback was that when the patients no longer needed me, I couldn't know how the animals were faring. I often felt like calling to see how they were.

Budgies were great favourites too. So long as they were caged I didn't mind, but a bird swooping round a room has never appealed to me. One patient, who knew more or less the time I would go to her, and on whose calendar I always marked the date of my next visit so that she could get her bird caged beforehand, would wait until I knocked on her door before trying to get the bird in. Then I would hear, 'Just a minute, dear. Don't open the door yet. Bobby's still flying around. I've nearly caught him. Oh, Bobby, you naughty boy, do what Mummy says and get into your cage. You're keeping Nurse waiting, but I shan't be long now, dear.' And so it went on, sometimes for ten minutes or more. I knew that if I went away the same rigmarole would still have happened. It was a dreadful waste of time. Until they moved away from the town I had a Christmas card from Bobby each year!

Another bird used to eye me as I attended his mistress, then give me his correct name and address, tell me he was a good boy, and do his party piece, 'Georgie Porgie, pudding and pie, kissed the girls, the girls, the girls...' until someone made a clicking sound, then he went on with the rest of the rhyme, but not as clearly as the first bit. He'd learned it from a repeatedly played record with a crack in it – when the needle was pushed on, the click was heard and on went the rhyme.

I knew one bird who pulled all his feathers out, living for years in a state of perpetual nudity and looking comically pathetic. His owners got advice and treatment from vets, but nothing did any good. He was a happy bird but very cold in the winter.

Sometimes it was difficult to appreciate how human a pet would become to its owner; if I didn't speak to her bird first, one patient would sit in glum silence and wouldn't let me touch her. Once I'd apologised to the bird for ignoring it, I could get on with my work – not that it took the slightest notice of me! In all other things she was a very sane, balanced soul, with a terrific sense of fun, but her bird was her life and had to be noticed.

There was one dreadful cat I met early on in this new life. Its habits really sickened me, but not its elderly owner, to whom I went twice a week. She had an early visit and was always at breakfast, surrounded by valuable antiques in the way of furniture, silver, glass, china etc, all so uncared for that it made me feel sad. The cutlery and porringer she used were solid silver, the cloth lovely damask, but stained and neglected. Very occasionally the cloth and serviettes were laundered, stiffly starched and gleaming white; they looked incongruous in the other filth. Just as I got her injection ready she would tell me to wait a bit as pussy wanted to be clean. The beastly thing would do its business on a piece of paper on the table. It was not always accurate in its aim, and the old lady would scrape it up with her own spoon! I was so nauseated that I had great difficulty in not adding to the mess by vomiting. She didn't turn a hair, but told the cat how clean it was! This animal never went outside, and had no litter tray, so where it passed water I could only guess from the awful smells and patches on the once beautiful carpets. Her help, who must have been paid well to endure it, used to bundle dirty clothes, table and bed linen all together and send it to a local laundry. I was very glad I didn't use a laundry, and when the patient died, that cat was one animal I didn't want to know about any more.

Death is part of nursing, since it is part of life, and contrary to general belief that we all 'get hardened to it', we had to learn to accept and accommodate it. At times it was most untimely, harder to bear than when it came as a friend to people worn out with pain and misery, and a source of thankfulness to loving relatives. Unexpected death happens at home as much as elsewhere, and involves police and coroners.

Once I was sent to a woman who hadn't registered with any local GP. She'd drifted anonymously over the country, ending up in a small bedsit. Another occupant in the multi-let house had heard her groaning, and though rebuffed when she offered help, had the sense to phone her own GP. I was called as I had many other patients nearby and was to report to the GP afterwards. The room was a small back one with a blazing gas fire, so hot I nearly passed out. In a tumbled bed was a very ill woman who had no intention of letting me touch her. All my suggestions were met with 'No', but she was in obvious discomfort, if not pain; her eyes shone fever bright. Under the pallor, her skin could be seen to have only recently been neglected. She must have been a most beautiful woman in the past, but now seemed alone and frightened. I was not allowed to see if her bed was wet, so I sat and held her hand as we talked. I couldn't actually count her pulse, but by moving my fingers a bit I could feel it was rapid and thready. The heat from the fire was dreadful, but she wanted it that way, so I put more money in the meter, left a glass of water and went off to the GP. I was unwilling to leave her but could do nothing by staying.

Talking it over with the doctor, I made him feel as concerned as I was, so he said he would visit, and if things were the same or worse the next day he would have to have her removed, against her will. No-one likes to have to do this, but some situations leave no other choice. A colleague called in the evening and had no more success than I. Next morning, as soon as I'd been to the diabetics, I went straight to this very worrying patient, wondering what I would find. The fire was still on, pouring out heat, the patient still in the tumbled bed, but she was dead. My first thought was one of regret that she had died alone, in a house where ten or more others lived. Then I felt that she had guarded her privacy so fiercely that perhaps death had been kind. At least she had not had to undergo forcible removal, so with mixed feelings I rang the GP and waited for officialdom to move in. The post-mortem report was death from a burst appendix, just one of many persons who slip through the net of a so-called welfare state. If she had any relatives, money or possessions, I never knew of course, but I did know it was a lonely, unnecessary death.

We often had eccentric patients who gave no hint to the GP that they would refuse our help, but not usually with such dire results as the previous one. One such was a very anaemic woman who had a dread of needles; by the state of her clothes this dread extended to the sewing variety also! Not even the GP, whom she trusted, could get a blood sample and she refused to swallow iron tablets, so I was asked to attempt to give her iron by injection, for it was much needed. The patient was there in the room, so was I, plus syringe, swab, ampoule of iron at the ready, but that's as far as I got. She said she would rather die than have any treatment. On one foot was an ulcer but it took me weeks to build up enough trust for her to let me treat it. Though relations slowly improved and the ulcer healed just as slowly, her health was getting worse. She was short of breath and putty-coloured, but still refused the life-saving iron in any form.

For as long as I was able, once the ulcer had healed, I used to call from time to time just to see how she was. She was a most prickly person, always trying to press money on me; when I refused, the hard won trust evaporated in hurt feelings. I was told that she didn't need the money, I pointed out that she did, to feed herself properly. I neither wanted nor needed her money, nor could I have taken it if I did. It was very uphill work dealing with her, I had to think of each word as I said it, but her reaction was never the same. So, when pressure of work and holidays meant I had no time for social calls, I was only half sorry to go past the house and not to stop. The house was like Fort Knox to get into, and I knew her landlady was a caring one who would always get the GP if she was worried. When I remembered I used to ask him how the poor soul was. I was jolted into awareness that she was still alive when I was asked to visit.

Going through all the rigmarole with various keys to get in, I found her more waxen than ever and if anything more unkempt and unwashed than before. Round one leg was a filthy bandage, I was to treat whatever was under it. From past experience I knew there would be nothing clean to use, so I had taken in clean towels as well as sterile dressing packs. I felt as though I'd prepared for anything. How very wrong I was! It took me a long time to get the patient on her bed to even start to undo the evil-smelling bandage, and once she was on the bed it took all my powers of persuasion and patience to get her to remove the awful stocking stuck over the bandage, as the first step in finding out what was underneath.

Eventually I got to the stage when I could start to soak off the stuck-on dressing – what it was I couldn't make out. She raised her leg high enough for me to put a waterproof sheet under it, and a roll of cotton wool to absorb the sterile water and antiseptic I intended to flush over. As I poured the first stream over the mess, out crawled several maggots! I was so horrified that for once I failed to hide my repugnance; my start was involuntary, but the job had to be done. Blessing the inventor of plastic gloves, I uncovered a heap of wriggling, obscene, fat white maggots, squirming all over the ulcer. My first feeling was to run away never to return, but common sense told me the maggots couldn't hurt me, only cause revulsion. Actually they had done a lot of good, eating away all the decaying muck and leaving fairly healthy pink flesh instead. All the same, it was a horrid job to make sure I'd got all the beastly things, not leaving even one behind to strike again. I put the whole lot into a chamber pot, put boiling water and disinfectant over it and flushed it away.

By this time I felt quite limp and had I been a smoker I would have lit up. All I could do was sit in the car until nausea retreated, then drive home for a quick bath and change of clothes before seeing my next patient. I felt that maggots were lurking round every corner and the buzz of a blowfly made me weak at the knees. I soon got over all that, and the ulcer healed, even though the woman got frailer. Then one day she fell downstairs and had to be taken to the place where she had refused to go for so long. Quite ironic really that before her anaemia could be finally investigated, she died.

10

How People Lived

Conditions in this, my home town, continued to amaze me, though most of the residents weren't local-born. So many people retired to places where they had enjoyed summer holidays, but had no roots. All too often the man died, leaving the widow without means enough to keep on the home they had had for a short time. With only her pension the widow often ended up in a small bedsit, or flatlet as they were more grandly called. These varied a lot; some were beautifully appointed, others a racket, high rents for ill-equipped, inconvenient rooms. Not all widows ended up like this of course, but many did, and we had a never-ending supply of them as patients, for many years. They were lonely, with no friends to help or prevent them from becoming prey to mental and physical ills. Churchgoers and card players fared better; they were able to meet like-minded people and start a new life.

Boarding houses and rest homes, private hotels and nursing homes flourished on money from the better off, or those less able to fend for themselves. In one of these so-called rest homes was a fully qualified nurse in charge, of an age when she could scarcely look after herself, let along others. Conditions had got so bad that there were only two left, the nurse (and her mangy dog) and another woman.

One hot Saturday, a window cleaner saw what he thought was a body on the floor, so he dialled 999. The 'body' was the non-nurse, who had fallen out of bed and was unable to get up; the old nurse had no power to lift her either. A nursing home was found for her and I was asked to attend the other one. A most peculiar smell greeted me, not just an unaired dirty one, but an underlying one I could not place; it wasn't from the dog either. A weak voice from upstairs answered my call, so I went up the filthy stairs of a large, well-built house, passable in appearance from the outside, but unspeakable inside.

The person I was looking for was in a large front bedroom, in a bed, which like the room was dirtier than anything I'd ever come across before. The inmate was equally dirty, with one leg grossly swollen and infected, the colour of her hair and skin obscured by dirt. The same smell was there and then I knew why – numerous rustlings heralded the eruption of dozens of mice! A very cultured voice asked me my business, so I answered with one eye on her and the other on the rustlers. I told her the doctor had asked me to see to her leg and make her clean and comfortable, and asked where I could find clean water, clothes, etc. I was hopeful! Actually the mice had driven every practical thought from my mind, the whole situation seemed impossible, and I didn't know where to start. Luckily it was too hot for a coat as there was no place I could have put it down on. 'Don't bother about me, dear. The Lord is going to take me,' said the patient, and without thinking how silly it sounded I said, 'Well, as far as I'm concerned the Lord will take you when you're clean, so I'll go and get a friend to help me.'

We'd arranged to meet after we'd both done our essential calls, and as I alone knew the enormity of the task awaiting us, I told my colleague to wait outside if she got there first. She joined me punctually, and I told her what I'd found inside. Unnoticed by me the first time, because I'd been too busy looking for a human occupant, was an upholstered sofa just inside the front hall, full of nests of squirming pink baby mice. Through an open door opposite was what in its palmy days had been the drawing room. The carpet had been eaten away in many places, all the furniture was full of mice in varying stages of growth, and there was a strong smell of them and stale urine. Stark panic threatened me, I'd always hated mice and here I was, surrounded! It was consoling that my friend was equally aghast at the hordes. Just one would have daunted me!

We ventured no further downstairs but went up, gathering our skirts round us, passing a fat mouse on the way. Boldly, as there were two of us, we looked into other rooms to see if things were different – what a hope! Beds were filthy and occupied by the inevitable mice, nesting in mattresses and pillows. There were foul-smelling commodes that had not been emptied for ages, floors were littered with chewed-up toilet paper and dirty knickers with the crotches eaten away. Feeling revulsion, we opened the last bedroom door, and there, amazingly, was a clean bed and room. Several mice were sleeping in the bed when we turned back the bedding, but at least we had a place for when our patient was clean. Bathroom and lavatory defied description, pipes had rusted through so that the water had been turned off, the pan was unflushed and full.

We were followed everywhere by the dog, who took no notice of the mice, or they of him. All over the place was food: opened packets of biscuits, cakes, sliced bread, butter, chocolate, tinned fruit and vegetables, from which the mice had easy pickings, spoiled for choice!

From the patient we learned that the gas and electricity meters were in the cupboard under the stairs, shilling in the slot ones. Until we'd put some money in we could get no hot water, but we had to brave the cupboard without a light. Luckily for us a consultant geriatrician turned up and he lent us his lighter, so armed with this flickering light and several coins, we dropped them into the first meter we found. The constant rustles and scamperings were unnerving, but we carried on and found an electric kettle with water in it, plugged it in, and then found too late, that the meter must have been the gas one. Still, we didn't want to face the unknown kitchen then, so we went back to the understair cupboard and put some shillings in the other meter and got the warm water for washing. During the weeks I'd accumulated towels, nighties and sheets etc. discarded by family, friends, and ex-patients. So we were able to get the old lady clean and into fresh clothes with her leg dressed. She was deeply ashamed of the way in which she had let herself go, but we made light of it and asked her about her nursing as we worked. She told us she'd nursed all sorts of illustrious people for the King's physicians and surgeons, mentioning many by name. We wondered if this was true and guessed that it was George V she meant; afterwards we found that it was quite true.

It was a job to get her to move to the one clean room – it was for her niece who came occasionally; it must have been very, very seldom! After all this she wanted a cup of tea. There was a packet in her room, but as a mouse had hopped out, I couldn't be sure that all the little black bits were tea! The milkman called each day so we had milk to give her; the only untainted food was a sealed tin of fancy biscuits, manna from heaven for us, but as it had been the other person's Christmas present she didn't want to open it. I told her that if it belonged to the Queen, I'd still open it. That raised the first laugh. With a promise to come back later, with tea and food, we both went home to bath and change, loath to do any more work.

I told my sister about the mice, so she put on her 'beetle crusher' shoes and came with me on my return visit. The fat mouse, still on the stairs and replete with food, was soon dispatched, then we went to find teapot and water for the promised cuppa. Green baize, largely eaten away, hung in shreds to the kitchen door in the hall, giving no hint of the horrors on the other side. Floor, chairs, table, draining board, plates and all surfaces were covered with thick grease, into which were embedded thousands of mice droppings. Open tins of fruit and vegetables had mould and drowned mice as contents. In the larder was a green, furry chicken carcase, mouldy and mousy food was everywhere on shelves and floor.

The worst discovery was dozens of milk bottles, full of dead, bloated mice. Even my stalwart sister blenched at these, but bravely took them out and smashed them so that no-one could use them again; one had five bodies in it. A cup had to be used to infuse the tea. The less we saw of the kitchen the better, so we drew a supply of water too. The mice were still hopping around the old lady; she said they were her friends so she couldn't kill them and go to her Maker with that on her conscience. I was glad that my sister had no such inhibitions; neither had I, it was my courage that was lacking!

I was determined to get out of the house before dusk, so after she had her tea and food, I left her with a bedpan to put under herself, a drink, the tin of biscuits and the dog and mice for company. It was most unsatisfactory to have to leave her in an unlocked house, with no proper food to hand, yet with all that contamination around there was no alternative. It was a Bank Holiday weekend too, so nothing official could be done until the next Tuesday. Luckily we found the outside lavatory intact. It was full of spiders, which though not appealing to me were secondary to mice.

My sister came with me again next morning. We were better prepared, so took a flask, bread and butter, marmalade and hard-boiled egg. We couldn't be sure if the milkman would leave all I'd asked him to, but found it there on the doorstep. At least we now felt more cheerful about food, if nothing else, and had also taken a large tin with a well-fitting lid. While I was seeing to the patient, my sister was busy breaking more milk bottles full of dead mice. So long as I was left alone I was beginning to take the live ones for granted, but I could never have coped without my sister, who was nothing whatsoever to do with the nursing service.

The visits and feeding continued. The squalor and smells no longer affected me as at first; besides, I felt confident that as soon as the authorities knew, something radical would be done. Tuesday morning found me in the office, but the reaction to my tale was far from expected. I was asked if I was refusing to nurse a patient! It wasn't the patient I was objecting to, it was the conditions. Even though I found out later that all home helps had refused to go back after one visit, no-one really wanted to believe me. In the end, it was grudgingly arranged that two sanitary inspectors would meet me at the house. They came punctually and spoke in that patronising voice men reserve for women they think are making a fuss about nothing. Once inside their attitude changed completely; they were more shattered than I had been from the first visit, and that's saying something! They said that not even wearing protective clothing would get them to work inside there.

Presumably their report was enough to get

something done, for when I went to do an evening call the place was locked up, with a secure padlock on the door. No-one volunteered any information to me about the patient's whereabouts, I had to ask, and took a very dim view of authority. I'd fed the patient for three days, given her bedding and nightclothes, been accused of not wanting to nurse a patient, and disbelieved about the appalling conditions, then not told that the patient had been removed to somewhere I knew nothing about. It made it much worse to realise that many people had known the squalid conditions were there. The house was sold and turned into 'luxury flats'! One day I looked through the window of the old drawing room. There were the same old floorboards, the same skirting with patches of wood filling up the mouse holes, and in memory I could smell, see and hear the mice; not even a free flat would have induced me to live there. A neighbour described the scene when the house was cleared as a vast funeral pyre in the front garden, cremating all the mice.

GPs often gave no real idea of the true state in which some people lived. In time I'd learned that, 'this patient is in a bit of a mess, do what you can', had to be translated into, 'the place is filthy, so is the patient, he or she is doubly incontinent, there's nothing to use and there is no-one else to do it'.

An address given me one afternoon was that of a large, double-fronted house, divided up into the inevitable flatlets, and just as inevitably a bell push and place for a name for each, with not one single name to be seen. The door was ajar, but not a sound was to be heard as my mouse house friend and I went in and asked if anyone was there. Eventually we traced the room we wanted by the smell. Against one wall was a single bed, covered with an old coat, newspapers and a blanket of dubious colour and cleanliness which hung over the edge, touching the floor. In the bed a mound moved a bit. From it came a very cultured 'top drawer' voice, then a tousled, grey head, a dirty, grey, lined face and two stick-like arms emerged. Two wardrobes, two chests of drawers, a cupboard, two chairs and a filthy sink with a draining board completed the room.

The smell was decidedly peculiar, but not mousy. Under the table and all over the place were empty port bottles. We kicked them as we moved from one spot to another. Under the bed were several chamber pots, full up with many days' supply of urine. So far all the words we'd heard were, 'Where's my port?' We started to look for towels and things and for hot water, and found a notice to the effect that hot water came on twice a day only. Of course we were too late for one and too early for the next. There was one miserable gas ring as the sole form of cooking appliance, very poor gas pressure and a battered saucepan with its bottom so out of shape it couldn't sit squarely on the ring. Each time we moved across the creaking floorboards the rickety table lurched and nearly shot the pan off the ring. There were stale, long-opened tins of powdered milk and coffee, with hard tops and damp underneath, so that little hissing jets of coffee gas, like miniature volcanoes, erupted every time the table was rocked.

Piles of rubbish as well as the bottles were everywhere as we searched in vain for any bed linen, towels and clothes, accompanied by the cry for port. The one towel we found was so stiff with dirt it wouldn't bend, so I went to my car again and drew on my collection, which was getting very depleted. Neither wardrobes nor chests of drawers held anything but dozens of parcels, newspaper packets of faeces, making the source of the smell clear to us; in some ways it was more horrifying than the mice.

A grocer gave us huge cartons into which we put all the parcels and rubbish, with the bottles apart as being non-burnable. A special collection was arranged for next morning, and all that could go into the incinerator did, including dozens of pound notes which, unknown to us, were folded among the papers on the bed. (We were told about these when it was too late!) All we'd wanted was to get the patient and her bed into a more wholesome state, so we had rolled up all the old covering and papers without inspection.

The plaintive cry for port went on non-stop, and the old lady wouldn't take any fluid we offered. To try and eke out the dwindling supply of bedding, I put an incontinence pad (a thin layer of polythene topped with several layers of soft paper) under her, until my next visit later on in the evening. I found the bed and all round it decorated with this pad, torn into little confetti-like pieces and scattered as far as she could reach. It took ages to collect every bit, and there was one avenue for keeping her bed dry, closed. In spite of no fluids she was always wet with concentrated urine; her poor kidneys were irritated by the lack of fluid. The cry for port came as soon as I went through the doorway, but by being as persuasive as I knew how to be, she swallowed a few spoons of tea on each visit. Wet bedding, twice a day, soon used up my store; it all stayed in a heap as there was no-one to wash the things. (Later on we had a home wash service, which collected, washed and returned.) Bedspreads, tablecloths, petticoats and anything else I could lay my hands on were soon swallowed up in this hopeless place, so a hospital bed had to be found. When the ambulance crew took her away she was still asking for her favourite tipple.

After this episode the patients I had were very normal in every way, but the lull didn't last long. A request came for me to call on an old man who had burned his leg, no more details than that, except for the address, right in the town, near the sea, in an area that had seen better days. The door knocker was a splendid brass one which gave a satisfying *thump, thud* as I used it. On the door too was a brass nameplate, with the correct name. Things were looking up!

A muffled voice answered mine. I paused to get adjusted to the dim light. This was an end-of-terrace house with no landing window. The meagre light from an open door at the end of the passage showed that all one side of it was stacked ceiling-high with newspapers. The light switch must have been on that wall for there was no sign of it on the other as I sidled along to where the voice had seemed to come from. The first room I came to was full of papers, any furniture was hidden from view. Getting more accustomed to the gloom, I went to the next room and there, surrounded by newspapers, was the man I'd come to see. He was sitting in an oasis, a paper-free zone, which held a table on which was a candlestick with candle, matches and a cup and plate, and an armchair, in which the man sat, hard against an old-fashioned paraffin heater. What a fire risk and potential death trap, I thought! But the old man didn't mind a bit. There was just enough room between the papers to get into an old scullery, where there was an anti-quated gas stove and sink. The lavatory was outside. If there was an upstairs lavatory or bathroom, I couldn't find out, the stairs were stacked with papers. The patient told me that he had slept and lived in the one room for ages, intending to read the papers, but things got out of hand with so many! You're telling me, I thought!

It was hard to find enough space to kneel down so as to see the burnt leg, and after I'd done so, I wished right heartily that I hadn't. The smell of human excreta is never very pleasant, but when one has just put one's knee into a pile of it, the smell and feel is sickening. I wiped as much off as I could with some of his toilet roll, but the window light was so obscured by dirt and the papers, that I wasn't very successful. Had I tried to find the light switch, which I was assured, with a wave of the hand in a vague direction, was 'just over there', I might have had an avalanche of papers marooning me along with the man, and that was unthinkable.

Somehow I got a dressing onto the luckily superficial burn, feeling most unprofessional with such unclean hands. I then went home to wash and change, leaving my clothes to soak, but for the rest of the day I imagined I still smelled of faeces.

Next day, knowing what to expect, I left my coat in the car and took a damp flannel, soap and towel for my own use. Even though he needed it badly, the man wouldn't submit to any form of washing.

At first he was very much on the defensive, knowing how peculiar his mode of living must seem to me, and he couldn't begin to understand why I was so worried about fire risks. When I really got to know him he relaxed and was a character, eccentric, but nice.

I reported the hazards in this house, but got nowhere. After all, there is no law against hoarding papers, even if they did fill the house. So far, according to his own standards, he'd looked after himself, and the milkman delivered all the essential foods, so as soon as the leg had healed, my visits ended. In the end the house did go up in flames, but the old man was rescued in time; I was very glad to know he was safe.

In this town is a lot of sheltered accommodation for the elderly, started in a small way by council bodies and churches; large houses were bought up and then converted into reasonably priced units for letting. Housing trusts then sprang up, increasing this type of housing. All was well as long as the occupants were self-sufficient, but the crunch came when illness or increasing old age made them lose this independence. Sometimes they needed 24-hour nursing, and they always needed food and drink, whether really ill or just under the weather. We were always being told that our job was to nurse, not to feed the patients, but if we had always obeyed the letter of the law, some of the poor old things would have fared very badly. It was impossible to match the demand for help with the supply; with so many people retiring to the coast, hospital beds were at a premium. I resented the fact that lifelong residents whose forebears had given money to build the town's hospital could not count on being given a bed when they needed one. We just had to nurse people in inadequate places until somewhere suitable could be found.

One of the first sheltered housing units provided by a church was in two semi-detached houses, with a communicating door put in, and a warden and husband were given a ground floor flat in one house. One house was in a good state when taken over, the other, having been lived in by one eccentric man, was in a mess and needed a long list of repairs and decorating. I had many patients there off and on through the years, mainly in the house that had started off in better nick. Then I was sent to see a woman in the other house who was very ill with pneumonia. Once again my nose picked up a smell which eluded me. I needed hotter water than that from the tap, so I put a kettle on and cleared the bedside table. The patient than asked me to pick up something she'd dropped the other side of her bed. As I leaned over I saw what looked like a mousetrap, so I bent further over to see. It was a mousetrap all right, with a mummified corpse! Goodness knows how long that mouse corpse had been there, but it was far too dry to be the source of the strange smell.

As I pulled back the bedclothes, small, flat, brown moving things met my eyes – bedbugs! Then my memory clicked back to India. I still had a mosquito net with stains no washing would remove from where I'd squashed my charming little bedfellows! Memory dredged up the pungent smell these horrible things exude. I'd had plenty experience of them, and judging by the scratches on the patient and the bloodstains on the sheets, so had she. Although bedbugs are slow movers, my wits were slower, all but one had gone out of sight as I gazed in astonishment; this one I squashed and put down sink, then realised that I'd no living proof of these horrible things.

In fact I almost doubted my own eyes. This was England in the 1960s, not rural India, the house was clean, not a slum, but I knew I'd not imagined the bugs and was very determined to catch a live specimen. I didn't tell my poor ill patient what I'd found, she said she'd been scratching herself for nights on end. I felt like doing it in broad daylight! By the time I'd got her clean and comfortable she was grey with exhaustion, so I left her to rest while I went to tell the warden about the bugs and mummified mouse. To my astonishment she was not in the least surprised about the bugs, she said someone had reported them and the mice to the local authority before she'd taken the post. She couldn't say if anything had been done. By this time I was speechless. It all seemed to be so casually accepted, whereas I was horrified and more determined than ever to find a live bug with which to confront the powers that be.

Next morning, I took an empty matchbox and duly caught a prime specimen to take to the MOH. Few people had every seen a bedbug so it was of great interest, even though that didn't do the patient any good. She needed much more nursing than I could provide, so she was moved to a nursing home. The room had to be fumigated before a new tenant took over. The picture rail was the bugs' hiding place, long before the house changed hands. Painting had merely sent them back into the plaster. Years later I had another patient there, in a different room, but with the same telltale scratches and bites. Whether more fumigation finally got rid of them I never knew, but knowing their persistence, a full stripping of the wall plaster was probably the only remedy.

11

Changes at Home and Visits Down Under

Changes in the methods of working practice to cover the town's sick folk were being discussed, in readiness for the unnecessary changes thought up by those with nothing better to do, in parliamentary and boundary reforms.

We knew that we were being taken over by the county. Even though our seniors objected to that way of defining it, that's the way we saw it, without pleasure. Our local authority was a good one to work for, we were happy as things were. Group Attachment was being mooted, all grades of nursing staff to work with a certain group of GPs, nursing their patients to the exclusion of all others, even if they lived in the same house. With so many multiple-unit houses, this looked like being a colossal waste of time and petrol and energy. For the time being we went on working on a geographical basis, responsible for all the sick people in our areas, no matter who their GPs were. There had been a gradual but definite increase in staff, more SENs and auxiliaries and, praise be, another male nurse! As these numbers had increased, so of course had our workload, and so many people still came here to retire that a continual strain was put on all resources.

The first real change was in our uniforms – no insignia of rank any more, causing consternation in some of the old hands; so long as my pay cheque reflected my grade, I didn't really bother. We had a choice of hats now, none particularly stylish compared with our old tricornes, but the supplier's rep had an amusing afternoon as we tried on the various types. He enjoyed it, if we didn't. Our old aprons had been the all-enveloping, hard-to-launder sort, but very useful in length when dealing with wet beds. The new tabards were easy to wash and wear but only three-quarters in length, leaving a very vulnerable stretch of frock below. At least our new speckled blue Harris tweed winter coats didn't pick up cat and dog hairs as easily as the old navy ones; however, it did seem an awful waste of good clothes, but as always we got used to the changes.

Our MOH was very keen on the Group Attachment Scheme, which was supposed to bring a much better liaison between GPs, nurses and health visitors, and result in a better service for the patients. Slowly it dawned on us that our familiar world was going to change and there was nothing we could do about it. We had heard so much about the future in the past, the far distant future it had seemed, but now that future was about to catch up with us.

We sorted out the lists of patients, handing some over regretfully, others with joy, and inheriting those from our colleagues in the same spirit. It was a most bewildering time for patients, who wanted to know where their own familiar nurse had gone, and a testing time for us. We were well aware that we had to build up new ties with GPs, patients and the surgery staff, yet continue to give the high level of patient care we had always given. On the whole, I had very little change of patients or GPs, as most of mine had come from those to whom I was now attached. Everyone seemed to be dashing all over the town, meeting colleagues in other practices in the same houses. Our mileages increased until we were spending more time driving than actually nursing. About a third of the staff thought it a good scheme, the rest, a sheer waste of time and valuable resources. For the first time, visibly at any rate, there was a division among us and we didn't like it.

While all this flux and turmoil continued, I went off to Australia, leaving the others to battle on.

The first ever International Domiciliary Nursing Congress was to be held in Melbourne, in their high summer, February. I applied for extra leave to add on to that owing me, quite willing to forgo my pay so that I could see friends as well as some of the land after going that far. But the local authority let me have my leave and my pay because I was paying my own fare, representing, with only three others, the UK Nursing Service. The local branch of the Royal College of Nursing generously paid my Congress fees.

I'd never flown in a large plane before, let alone realised that it could be a bus ride to dispersal point from the terminal. The jumbo looked so huge it seemed impossible that it could ever get airborne, but it did.

I had three seats to myself, so I was able to stretch out and doze a bit. Flying over India was very nostalgic, and it was surprising to see so much water below; when living there water seemed very poorly supplied. Landing in Calcutta with its familiar sounds and smells was quite intoxicating. Flying on to Singapore, the sea below was a deep blue, with cotton wool swabs as clouds. Home was far away, literally and mentally. Dozens of Chinese and Malaysian students embarked at Singapore, so I lost my other seats. All were off to Melbourne University, the two next to me on their first trip. Both were very friendly, but one had dreadful catarrh; the sniff, snort, blow variety, very trying to listen to. Mealtime was a revelation, all the courses were piled up together, crowned with the roll and butter. The lads were very dextrous with knife and fork, solemnly cutting through the pyramid of foods. I felt a bit squeamish when a flake of salmon got eaten on the same fork prong as custard, but it made compulsive watching.

They asked me how to fill in the forms, even as to what to put down about the value of clothes and books in their luggage. Considering I'd no idea what they owned and had only just met them, it was too tall an order for me. One fell asleep on my shoulder, the clear nose one, so I was lucky!

A doctor friend met me at the airport, and it was good to see a well-remembered face at the end of such a long journey. I had several days in a Melbourne motel before going to the university hostel for the Congress.

There were delegates from all round the world, all housed in the various hostels. The other three from the UK were two from Nottingham and the other from Jersey; they had the bare travelling and Congress time, their fares having been paid by various fund-raising efforts, so I was glad I was paying my own way. It seemed dreadful to come all that distance, to such a fascinating land, and have no time to see much of it.

My room was in a very spartan men's hostel, with rows of washbasins and no privacy for middle-aged women, as most of us were. The lack of catches on the two shower cubicle doors was soon put right with pieces of string. I suppose the men did no ironing, for there wasn't one in the place.

Our things had been packed so many miles and hours away that they needed attention. I was lucky in having friends in the city and could borrow whatever I needed.

The Australians were of course the largest contingent, and those in my hostel were most vociferous in their many complaints. After all, they were in their own country and could complain when we could not, but it didn't produce an iron. Food in that country, so rich in meat, fruit and vegetables, was most unsuitable; on one of the hottest days of the year we had boiled beef and carrots with dumplings, followed by steamed pudding.

Still, it was good to talk and exchange ideas, to get to know nurses from other countries. We from the UK, when talking to others, realised how favoured our working conditions were compared with some. Our relationships with our GPs were on a personal level, whereas we were told that some of those in Australia didn't even know their nurses' names. There seemed no reason to doubt this, but we were amazed.

Some speakers were deadly dull, but others were outstanding, two in particular. One, a cancer specialist from London, the second an unassuming girl from the outback who worked among the Aboriginal tribes. Although she could call on the Flying Doctor Service, most decisions had to be taken by her, and she had to be self-reliant in everything, even in the repair and upkeep of her Land Rover. The air-conditioning in the hall had incurable hiccups so was useless, but we all forgot the heat as we listened to this thin young nurse telling her everyday story, which to us was far from commonplace. Our applause took her by surprise, she could genuinely see nothing unusual in her story.

We had a garden party given in our honour by the State Governor on a sweltering day. We wilted in our glad rags in a most lovely house and gardens, many of the guests observing protocol and wearing gloves. The very thought made me even hotter.

Other outings were laid on too, whetting my appetite for seeing more of the country. The Congress ended with a banquet; somehow everybody got their long frocks uncreased, many hairdressers made a small fortune and the food amply made up for all the mediocrity we'd endured before. All in all it was a thoroughly worthwhile experience.

As for me, I saw as much of the country as I could, all the friends I could too, including one who had seen the war years with me in India, then I went to New Zealand to see another friend from those far-off days and fell in love with that country too, but my leave was coming to the end. So, back to Australia to reclaim things left with friends there and board a plane for the long trip home, with no idea that I should ever go that way again.

Once back home, feeling the cold of a late spring, with jet lag I'd not got over because pressure of work had sent me back two days earlier than had been arranged before I left for Australia, it was desperately hard to settle again. I'd been in hotter weather than I'd known for over 20 years, and though not really discontented, I had been jolted out of normal life. Time was the only cure, I knew. The driving all over the town on the Group Attachment Scheme was still going on, adding to my uncertainty.

For a little while we went back to our old territorial working, but in the end, as we knew he would, the MOH had his own way and insisted on our making the group scheme work. This second go was far better planned than the first, so we settled down again.

Community nurses were beginning to go for specialised training courses, ready for the time when all accepted for working in the Community Nursing Service had to have this extra qualification. At first two at a time were sent; some, including me, opted out, knowing that before everyone at present employed had gone on the course, we'd be retired. The scheme had to be accelerated once it was realised how long it would take for all the staff to have this training.

In all these changes the main type of our patients stayed the same – elderly, living alone, or very old couples – at least that is how it was in our practice. But suddenly numbers, or so it seemed, started to drop off, and we wondered why. Then understanding dawned. Many of the large, sub-divided houses were being sold for demolition and the sites developed for luxury blocks of flats well beyond the means of our average patients' incomes. Great distress was caused in many cases, for they had no security of tenure; the owners didn't care where the displaced went so long as they got their fat profits. Presumably many drifted away to other towns. The face of the town was being altered out of recognition; some of the changes were sheer vandalism of beautiful old property, in the guise of progress. The dirty patients became fewer, some died, some went into rest homes, and, more rarely, families assumed a long-forgotten responsibility.

Eccentric behaviour still cropped up. One household was really strange. The man was a sort of aristocratic failure, never succeeding in anything he tried to do, but he knew all there was to know about everything, including nursing. We were told how to nurse not only his wife, but all our other patients he had never, and would never, meet! His wife had a progressive disease which made her almost bedridden, but neither would admit to this illness, we were told it was perpetual tiredness. They held very decided views about food, cooking utensils and drink. Only green tea was drunk, no aluminium was allowed in the house and a saucerful of red boiled linseed was eaten every day by both. I was offered some as being good for my bowels also!

It was rather tiring dealing with him and the two pekes, who resided on the wife's bed. They had to be coaxed off, twice a day, before we could start. A certain ritual had to be observed with a long rigmarole told to the dogs as to why they had to be moved;

hours were wasted every day. While all this was going on we could have been getting the hot water, which would have been accepted in any other house but this. If we did presume to get it the man would take it out, throw it away and then make us wait even longer for the bowlful. He tried to dictate which nurse should call when one had rashly pointed out the time we wasted on the non-nursing rituals. I, as the one who went most regularly, alas pointed out that whoever was on evening calls would attend to his wife or no-one. It wasn't a privilege to attend his wife, as he thought.

All the hair combings from the dogs were kept in bags for weaving into wool, in the event of another war, and all their excreta bagged up and stored in an outside shed, to be used as manure when he had a proper garden! He had never done anything physical in his prime, so what chance of it in frail old age? Our times of visiting only varied by minutes, according to the traffic and finding a parking place, but not once were the dogs off the bed ready for us to get on. They were both out of touch with real life, but so dogmatic that after a visit there wasn't one of us that didn't feel drained of thought and energy. A constant verbal barrage is very wearing.

Dietary habits of patients I've nursed in their homes would make a remarkable cookery book – that household would have a section all to itself.

Some washing habits too were unusual, some too nauseating to record, but I had once to visit a woman who had fallen in the bathroom and was severely shaken and bruised. In her bathroom was a large packet of Persil, she said she must have put too much in the water, making it so slippery that she'd fallen! Her hair was beautifully soft and white, washed in the same powder, thus proving the truth of TV ads, but I'm sure the makers never thought of applying their vaunted whiteness to human hair and skin. One patient of long standing always apologised for only having 'cooking soap' for me to wash my hands with.

The name 'district nurse' was now obsolete, like so many other well-tried and tested titles. We were now community staff. SRNs were officially sisters and SENs nurses. The patients, bless their hearts, continued to call us nurse, dear, ducks, or anything they thought of. Terms like top management or middle management sounded more like factory working than nursing.

Student nurses were now being given the option of doing two out of three choices during their third year. For six weeks they could choose either obstetrics, psychiatric or community nursing, so that every so often we would have students out with us. This was an eye-opener to most, who had never been deprived of anything from babyhood onwards. Now they were in direct contact in people's homes, so different from hospital nursing, with people who could dredge up from their memories all sorts of things which added to the wider education of the young ones.

They began to see the elderly as individuals, not statistics who were blocking the valuable hospital beds. Problems, social as well as nursing, were seen in the same context, and most of the students became very interested in our sort of nursing. Meeting members of the family in the home was very different from seeing them at a hospital bed. The patients enjoyed these young ones, even if they got muddled by the constant change. One old lady, to whom I'd been going for years, told me that much as she liked one student, she really thought I should let her get a lot more experience before leaving her in charge. By the time she had had several students visit her with me she was in a complete muddle, even though I'd warned each time of a change of girl. One was a very pretty girl, so the next day, when I was on my own, the old lady asked me if she took after her father, my husband, saying as she looked at me, 'She must look like him, for she was lovely!' To this I heartily agreed, but couldn't convince her that all these girls, with such different looks, were not my daughters. She often asked how my girls were, obviously thinking me a most unfeeling mother when I couldn't even tell her where they were. I always told the students of her thoughts before we went in, so that they could get over the merriment first; they were very amused.

I had another trip to Australia and New Zealand by saving up my whole year's holiday entitlement (it nearly killed me to have no break in a busy year). Forest fires and a glacier were things I saw that had never been in my most wildest moments of imagination; the hard year without holiday was well worth it. On my return there were yet more discussions about another change in the uniforms for the community staff. It suddenly came home to me that these things were not going to affect me, my present uniform would see me out, as I was looking forward to the reality of retirement.

All the staff, nursing and otherwise, who were attached to the practice were invited to Christmas parties, given in turn in some of the GPs' homes, so perhaps there were some advantages in group attachment though it took me a long time to acknowledge them. We did present a more united front in patient care, with wider horizons than in the old way of working. The doctors told me that they were giving me a retirement party; I thought how this would surprise the Australian nurses whose names were not known by the GPs.

My last year was a very busy one, no letting up in deference to age! Good health and a largely contented nature never stood me in better stead than then, and the thought of finishing must have spurred me on too. I had hoped for an easy winter, weather-wise, for this last one, with no driving from A to Z in swirling snow or fog, but this was not to be. We had a short, sharp spell, the worst coming just before it was time to set out for the evening calls. The snow, which had been falling half-heartedly, started to come down in earnest. My calls were all over the town, none could be omitted. Town traffic had left the roads in treacherous slush and ice, the snow giving an eerie light as it swirled around. Wipers were of little use as it was very sticky snow. Daylight had more or less finished by the time my round was done, even though I'd started a bit earlier. One patient was most upset that I'd got to her a little before the normal time, telling me that she could not see what difference a bit of snow made, after all, I was in a car! I bit back the words of reply which came readily to mind.

Feeling relieved that I was on my way home and that the next day I was off duty, I drove cautiously along the snow-packed, icy roads. Knowing that I was nearing my turning, I dropped to a crawl to negotiate the bend, enraging a lad who was in a clapped-out car, much too close behind me in any weather and going far too fast in such road conditions. He overtook me at speed with an angry glower of impatience which soon changed to alarm as he skidded across the road, shooting up the other half of my road, turning round full circle and onto the pavement before he could stop. It was a mercy no other car was coming in either direction. I saw that he was unhurt but had neither patience nor energy to slither across two roads just to tell him I was alive after years of driving because I'd been careful when fools were around. I don't think somehow that would have gone down very well. The snow was washed away by rain on my day off and we had no more then.

Routine work went on, my final weeks coinciding with the end of our year. So for the last time I transferred, ready for 1st April, the names of patients into the register. I was unbelievably visiting patients to whom I'd been going for ages, for the last time, saying goodbye with a sense of un-reality. Retirement parties and presentations went off with a feeling of detachment, as though someone else in my body was going through the motions.

Waking up at the same time as I'd done for years, my first day of freedom was just like the start of a normal holiday. It took about two weeks before I really accepted the fact that I didn't have to get up and go to work ever again.

The publishers hope that this book has given you enjoyable reading. Large Print Books are especially designed to be as easy to see and hold as possible. If you wish a complete list of our books please ask at your local library or write directly to:

Dales Large Print Books
Magna House, Long Preston,
Skipton, North Yorkshire.
BD23 4ND